Paul's Letter
to the Romans

Paul's Letter to the Romans

A Reader-Response Commentary

John Paul Heil

PAULIST PRESS
New York • Mahwah

Maps by Frank Sabbate, C.S.P.

Book design by Nighthawk Design.

Library of Congress Cataloging-in-Publication Data

Heil, John Paul.
    Paul's letter to the Romans.

    Bibliography: p.
    Includes index.
    1. Bible. N.T. Romans—Commentaries. I. Title.
BS2665.3.H4   1987   227′.1977   87-7030
ISBN 0-8091-2898-5 (pbk.)

Published by Paulist Press
997 Macarthur Boulevard
Mahwah, N.J. 07430

Printed and bound in the United States of America

Contents

Table of Sigla

NovTSup   Novum Testamentum, Supplements

NTS   *New Testament Studies*

RSR   *Recherches de science religieuse*

SBLDS   Society of Biblical Literature Dissertation Series

SBT   Studies in Biblical Theology

ScrB   *Scripture Bulletin*

SNTSMS   Society for New Testament Studies Monograph Series

ST   *Studia theologica*

Str-B   H. Strack and P. Billerbeck, *Kommentar zum Neuen Testament*

TDNT   G. Kittel and G. Friedrich (eds.), *Theological Dictionary of the New Testament*

VD   *Verbum domini*

WMANT   Wissenschaftliche Monographien zum Alten und Neuen Testament

WTJ   *Westminster Theological Journal*

WUNT   Wissenschaftliche Untersuchungen zum Neuen Testament

ZNW   *Zeitschrift für neutestamentliche Wissenschaft*

ZTK   *Zeitschrift für Theologie und Kirche*

Chapter I

Introduction

A. Reader-Response Approach

Why another commentary on Romans? This question is particularly relevant since there is certainly no dearth of commentaries on Paul's Letter to the Romans. The following, however, will take a somewhat different approach than most commentaries. We will attempt a primarily literary, rhetorical, "reader-response" avenue to the text of this most significant Pauline document.

Our method treats Romans as a literary communication employing rhetorical devices and means of argumentation intended to persuade its recipients to feel, think or act in certain ways. It focuses upon what mental moves or responses Paul as the epistolary author is trying to evoke from his intended Roman audience through the rhetoric of the letter. It seeks to articulate how the text of Romans as a literary, rhetorical communication "works" upon, what persuasive effects it is intended to have upon, its implied readers.

By mentally placing ourselves in the position of the implied reader(s) of the text and making the responses that the process of reading or listening to it demands or requires, we hope to experience more precisely and fully what this epistle is meant to communicate. This "reader-response" approach will be the guiding principle of the commentary.

B. Apocalyptic-Eschatological Framework of Paul's Thought

Before turning to the text of the epistle we need to situate its historical background and cultural-religious environment. In general

1

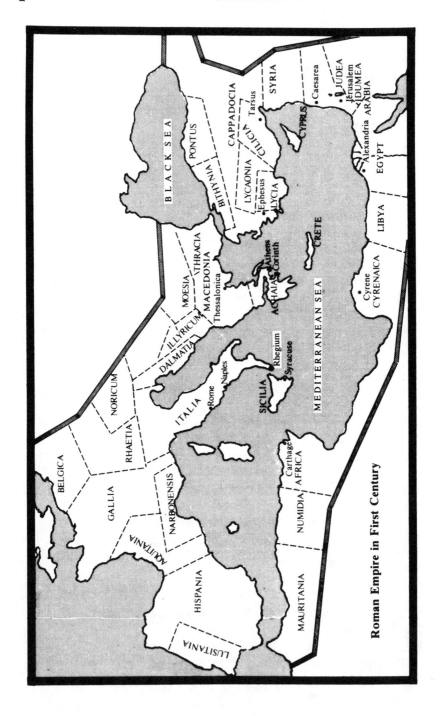

Roman Empire in First Century

both Paul and his Roman audience were inhabitants of the Greco-Roman empire that dominated the Mediterranean area during the first century. More specifically they both breathed the air of the apocalyptic-eschatological atmosphere that permeated first century Judaism whether in Palestine or in the many diaspora communities strewn throughout the Mediterranean regions.

This Jewish apocalyptic-eschatology accounts for the world view which is presupposed and shared by the author and audience of Romans. It forms the fabric of the "epistolary world" created by the text and in which the communication of the letter takes place. And so it behooves us to review those key apocalyptic-eschatological beliefs and concepts which will help us to understand Paul's way of thinking and point of view in the letter.

1. *Suffering and the Demonic Power of Evil*

In the course of Jewish history after the Babylonian Exile and especially in the few centuries preceding the Christian era certain developments in Jewish thinking about God, the universe and the problem of suffering and evil took place. God seemed to become more and more distant from his creation and from his people while experiences of persecution, oppression, suffering and evil became more and more acute. It was as if the powers of evil had wrested control of the cosmos from God. Everything and everyone seemed to live under the unavoidable influence of demonic powers.

2. *God's Secret Plan for the "End-Time"*

But despite this universal grip of evil the belief and hope remained strong that God's unforgettable faithfulness to his creation and people would ultimately prevail. According to this way of thinking, generally termed "apocalyptic-eschatology," God has a hidden plan for the universe whose secrets or "mysteries" he reveals to specially chosen people. God's secret plan concerns the inevitable cosmic upheaval and transformation that will bring about the "end" of time. "This age" of intense distress will very soon be followed by "the age to come," the eschatological or "end"-time when God will triumphantly fulfill his abiding purpose and promises.

3. *God's Universal Judgment*

One of the key ways in which God will manifest his truthfulness and fidelity by correcting or rectifying what has gone wrong in creation will be *judgment.* At the end of days there will be some sort of universal judgment in which those who are wicked will justly experience the full force of God's anger or "wrath" and those who are good or "righteous" will be "saved" from God's wrath and appropriately rewarded. This rectifying and salvific activity of God will extend to the whole universe, so that the "old" created order will be restored or recreated into a "new" creation.

4. The Cosmic, Temporal and Social Dimensions of Apocalyptic-Eschatological Dualism

Apocalyptic-eschatology is thus characterized by a strictly dualistic view of reality with cosmic, temporal and social dimensions:

APOCALYPTIC-ESCHATOLOGICAL DUALISM

Cosmic:	heavenly realm	vs.	earthly realm
	God	vs.	demonic powers
Temporal:	age to come	vs.	this age
	new creation	vs.	old creation
Social:	good	vs.	wicked
	elect	vs.	world
	righteous	vs.	unrighteous

5. Paul's Apocalyptic-Eschatological Thought

Paul's thought and language are thoroughly apocalyptic-eschatological in character. He explains the universal experiences of sinfulness and death in terms of apocalyptic powers which totally dominate and doom all of creation. "Sin" and "Death" are the archenemies which determine both the present realm and the final destiny of human existence. But God has now victoriously shattered the destructive dominion of these evil powers by the death and resurrection of his own Son, Jesus Christ.

The end-time and new age of God's rectifying and salvific activity has finally and definitively burst upon the cosmic arena. God has now openly revealed his hidden plan of salvation for all. No longer must the created universe be subjugated to the bondage of Sin and Death. The Creator has established a new relationship with his creation. All people can accept this new relationship by placing their trust in the God who raised Jesus from the realm of death.

All who so believe live within the realm of God's new relationship of rectifying faithfulness dominated by the power of God's Spirit. This faith gives them the sure hope of being saved from God's furious wrath and final condemnation to eschatological death in the last judgment. They can and should already live in accord with their final destiny, God's eternal life.

In general and summary terms this describes the apocalyptic-eschatological "good news" or gospel Paul has been commissioned by God to preach to all peoples. It is this apocalyptic-eschatological revelation of God that provides us with Paul's overall point of view in his Letter to the Romans.[1]

C. Paul as the Epistolary Author

Who is this Paul and what do we need to know about him in order to understand his Letter to the Romans? By birth Paul was a diaspora Jew and Roman citizen born in the city of Tarsus which was in Cilicia, a region of Asia Minor (present day Turkey) (Acts 21:39). He was well-educated in and strictly observant of the ways of the Jewish religion (Acts 22:3). After fiercely persecuting the Christian movement, Paul, based upon a personal "conversion" experience of the risen Lord Jesus, became not only a Christian but a great champion of the Christian gospel, the renowned "apostle to the Gentiles."

1. Paul's Missionary Career and Letters

According to the Acts of the Apostles Paul enjoyed considerable missionary success, establishing many Christian communities throughout the Mediterranean area. In the course of this missionary activity Paul wrote various letters to at least some of these communities. The New Testament contains thirteen epistles directly attributed to Paul. Not all of these, however, were actually written by Paul. There are seven which are generally agreed to be genuine Pauline epistles: Romans, 1 Corinthians, 2 Corinthians, Galatians, Philippians, Philemon and 1 Thessalonians. Three others, the so-called "deutero-Pauline" epistles, are believed to have been written either by Paul or by close associates of Paul: Colossians, Ephesians and 2 Thessalonians. Another three can be called pseudo-Pauline epistles, as they are considered to be later compositions which claim the prestige of Pauline

authorship. They are the so-called "Pastoral Epistles": 1 Timothy, 2
Timothy and Titus.[2]

2. Paul's Letter to the Christians at Rome

The Letter to the Romans stands as the last in the series of genuine
Pauline epistles that we have. It may well have been written during
Paul's final sojourn in Corinth perhaps in 55-56 A.D. Paul composed
it at an important turning point in his illustrious missionary career. He
had already proclaimed the gospel and founded various Christian
communities throughout the Mediterranean area bounded by Jerusalem, the mother Church, in the east and by Illyricum (presently in
Yugoslavia) in the west (Rom 15:19).

As he writes the Letter, Paul, apostle to all nations, hopes to bring
the gospel to Spain in the far western regions of the Roman Empire.
But before he can do that, he must successfully deliver the monetary
contribution of the Christian communities of Macedonia and Achaia
to the poor among the Christians of the mother Church of Jerusalem
(Rom 15:23–29).

The Christian community at Rome, although not founded by
Paul, has an important role to play in all of this. He writes to them for
the following reasons. First, aware of their well-known Christian faith,
Paul has for a long time ardently desired to visit them but has been
prevented from doing so (Rom 1:8–10; 15:22). Although they are already Christian believers, Paul wants to present his gospel to them as
members of all the peoples, whom he is obliged to evangelize (Rom
1:5–6, 13–15). By presenting his gospel in Rome Paul can strengthen
and encourage the faith they share with him (Rom 1:11–12). The body
of the Letter (Rom 1:16–15:13) is intended to fulfill this purpose for
Paul.

Second, the Letter is meant to prepare the Roman Christians for
Paul's actual visit, when they can, in turn, encourage and spiritually
refresh him (by doing what he advises them in the Letter) before ma-
terially supporting his missionary endeavor toward Spain (Rom 15:24,
32).

Third, through the Letter Paul solicits the prayerful support of
the Roman Christians who can thereby struggle along with him in his
crucial attempt to have the collection well and properly accepted by the
mother Church of Jerusalem (Rom 15:30–32).

This then sketches the occasion for the Letter and the historical
situation of Paul as its author.

D. Roman Christians as the Epistolary Audience

What do we know about the historical situation of Paul's intended Roman audience?

1. Christians in Jewish Synagogues at Rome

At the time of Paul there were a number of Jewish synagogue communities existing within the large, diverse and cosmopolitan city of Rome, the administrative center of the Empire. Exactly how Christianity came to Rome is unclear. But in all likelihood it originated within the established network of Roman Jewish synagogues.

2. Expulsion of Jews from Rome

According to the Roman biographer Suetonius (*Vita Claudii,* 25.4), during the reign of the emperor Claudius and sometime between 41 and 49 A.D., riots erupted among the Jews because of a certain "Chrestus" (variant spelling of "Christus"). This may reflect agitation between the followers of Christ and other Jews. As a result of this disturbance many Jews were expelled from Rome.

Among those expelled were the Jewish Christians Aquila and his wife Prisca, who became close associates and co-workers of Paul at Corinth (Acts 18:2). Probably after the death of Claudius (54 A.D.) when Jewish exiles could return to Rome, they came back and were present there when Paul wrote the Letter (Rom 16:3).

3. Jewish and Gentile Christians at Rome

Perhaps Claudius' expulsion of Jews from Rome occasioned Christians to leave the Jewish synagogues and establish their own communities, based in the households of people like Aquila, Aristobulus, Narcissus and Philologus, mentioned in the Letter as heads of households (Rom 16:3, 10, 11, 15). It may have been a time of considerable increase in the number of Gentile Christians. At any rate, when Romans was written, Christianity at Rome was composed of both Gentile and Jewish Christians coexisting either within the synagogues or as separate house churches or both.[3]

Paul's Letter to the Romans implies a mixed Christian community/communities of Jews and Gentiles as its audience, whose faith as a whole is well-known and competent (Rom 1:8; 15:14). Included within this implied audience are those whom Paul designates "strong" in faith and those whom he calls "weak" in faith with regard to a troubling religious-cultural issue involving the eating or non-eating of certain foods and the observing or non-observing of certain days (Rom 14:1–15:13). In addition, according to Romans 16 quite a number of Paul's fellow missionary workers and close associates now reside among his Roman audience (Rom 16:1–15).[4] This Jewish and Gentile mixture of Christians depicts the general sociological composition of the Letter's audience in itself.

4. The Various Groups Involved in Romans

To gain a fuller delineation of the Roman audience, however, it is helpful to consider other sociological groupings involved in the Letter. There are several sociological entities which are distinct from, yet in one way or another related to, Paul's intended Roman readers. In the Letter Paul speaks to his readers as distinct from yet related to certain Christian and certain non-Christian groups:

SOCIOLOGICAL GROUPINGS IN ROMANS

Christian

The mother Church of Jerusalem (Rom 15:19, 25–32)

Pauline communities between Jerusalem and Illyricum, e.g. in Macedonia and Achaia (Rom 15:19, 26; 16:4, 16)

Paul's co-workers and close associates (Rom 16)

Non-Christian

Jews who do not yet believe in the gospel (Rom 3:1–8; 9–11)

Gentiles—"Greeks and barbarians"—who have not yet heard the gospel (Rom 1:1–15; 15:14–29)

Ruling governmental authorities (Rom 13:1–7)

Christian and/or Non-Christian

Miscellaneous enemies/persecutors/opponents (Rom 8:31–39; 12:14–21; 16:17–20)

These are the various groups which, as we will see in more detail later, have particular roles to play in the Letter and which further define the sociological situation of our Epistle's Roman audience.

E. The Roman Letter as a Literary-Rhetorical Communication

Before we can profitably plunge into the text of Romans, we need to consider its nature and character as a literary-rhetorical communication between its author and intended audience.

1. Paul's Rhetorical Manner and Style

In general we may characterize Romans as a theological, literary-rhetorical argumentation and demonstration aimed at persuading its audience to accept the viewpoint of its author. In Romans Paul adopts and adapts certain rhetorical strategies, tactics and means of argumentation current in his day and familiar to his intended audience.

For example, Paul employs his own adaptation of the Cynic-Stoic diatribe, in which the author attempts to illustrate his argumentative points and drive home his persuasions by rhetorically indicting, interrogating and dialoguing with an imaginary interlocutor, before the eyes and for the benefit of his audience.[5] Along with and within this general diatribal manner of argumentation Paul utilizes a variety of literary-rhetorical devices and techniques to effectively evoke the appropriate mental, emotional and attitudinal responses needed to win over his audience. These are the kinds of responses we will be concerned to determine and pursue in our "reader-response" approach to Romans.

2. Paul's Use of Scripture

The Letter's rhetorical communication presupposes a basic knowledge of the Jewish "Old Testament" scriptures. Indeed, Paul's argumentation largely depends upon his own authoritative interpretation and use of the scriptures to cogently demonstrate the apocalyptic-eschatological revelation of God's secret and hidden plan for universal salvation. The rhetoric of our Epistle both explicitly and implicitly depends upon the accepted authority of God's written word.

The Jewish synagogal background of Paul's audience would have assured their fundamental familiarity with the holy scriptures. Even Gentile Christians, many of whom were undoubtedly "God-fearers," proselytes or sympathizing adherents of the synagogue, could easily have acquired the scriptural acquaintance needed to understand Paul's rather rudimentary application of the scriptures in his argumentation. In fact, for its intended audience Paul's method of argumentation and logic required no special, technical, private or esoteric training, but rather possessed a public and open character which would have been readily comprehensible to both Jew and Gentile, Greek and barbarian.[6]

3. The Epistolary Author and His Desired Responses from the Implied Readership

The Paul we encounter in Romans is the authoritative epistolary author who controls the argument, the rhetorical communicator bent upon swaying his audience to his own convictions and viewpoints. The audience we meet in Romans is not a real or actual Roman audience but an implied or intended epistolary audience created and established by the author Paul through the text of the Epistle. Although Paul surely meant to address a real, historical Roman Christian audience, he did so by characterizing, imagining and placing them in certain rhetorical positions by means of the text of the Epistle.

It is the desired responses of this imaginary or implied audience that will be the focus of our "reader-response" approach to the text of Romans. We will be concerned to determine not how the actual, historical Roman audience may have responded in hearing or reading the Letter, but how the imaginary, implied audience is required or meant to respond to the Letter's rhetorical communication.

Calculating the responses of this implied audience, then, is not a matter of historical or subjective speculation but is controlled by rhetorical analysis of the text. The implied audience or reader is also distinguished from ourselves as actual contemporary readers. We are called upon and challenged to assume the position of the implied audience of the text if we wish to fully experience the emotional, attitudinal and mental persuasions the Letter is intended to communicate. By experiencing its desired rhetorical effects we can better comprehend and appreciate the Letter's message. This will be the challenge of our commentary.[7]

F. Literary-Structural Overview of the Letter

Before we commence our reading of Romans we want to take a summary glance at its overall literary structure and main flow of thought. This is the outline we will follow in the commentary:

OUTLINE OF ROMANS

I. Rom 1:1–17: Setting the framework for the presentation of Paul's Gospel to the audience of the Letter.
   A. Paul introduces himself and greets the Christians at Rome (1:1–7).
   B. Paul's driving desire to visit and evangelize the Romans (1:8–15).
   C. Paul and the Gospel of Power (1:16–17).

II. Rom 1:18–3:20: Paul relates his audience to the situation of:
   A. The "ungodly" (1:18–32).
   B. The morally "upright" (2:1–16).
   C. The "upright" Jew (2:17–3:8).
   D. All sinners (3:9–20).

III. Rom 3:21–4:25: Paul relates his audience to the situation of:
   A. All who are now justified by God apart from the Law (3:21–31).
   B. Abraham, the father in faith and hope of Christian Gentiles and Jews (4:1–25).

IV. Rom 5:1–8:39: Paul encourages his audience by presenting the consequences of being justified by faith.
   A. Our present peace, grace and hope for future glory (5:1–11).
   B. Our present situation of grace and hope for Life more than surpasses our former situation of sinfulness leading to Death (5:12–21).
   C. We are now able to live in freedom from the dominion of Sin (6:1–14).
   D. We must now live in freedom from the dominion of Sin (6:15–23).
   E. We are now freed from the imprisonment of the Law to serve God in the newness of the Spirit (7:1–6).
   F. The Law became the "Law" of Sin and Death for each of us (7:7–25).
   G. But the "Law" of the Spirit of Life has freed each of us from the "Law" of Sin and Death (8:1–17).
   H. We can be absolutely assured that our future glory will far surpass our present sufferings (8:18–39).

V. Rom 9:1–11:36: Paul persuades his audience that presently unbelieving Israel will be saved.
   A. Paul shares with his audience his deep concern for his fellow Israelites (9:1–5).

    B.   But the word of God has not failed with regard to Israel (9:6–29).

    C.   Faith is still available to Israel (9:30–10:21).

    D.   The present unbelief of Israel is interrelated to the faith of Christians (11:1–24).

    E.   Paul proclaims his hope that all Israel will be saved so that God might have mercy on us all (11:25–36).

VI. Rom 12:1–15:13: Paul exhorts his audience to live the new life God has given them.

    A.   Rom 12:1–13:14: Live now in accord with your hope for the future.

        1.   Give yourselves over to a new life pleasing to God (12:1–2).

        2.   Use your various charisms for the harmonious functioning of the community (12:3–8).

        3.   Practice communal love (12:9–21).

        4.   Obey governing authorities (13:1–7).

        5.   Love one another (13:8–10).

        6.   Now is the time to live this new life as our future salvation is coming ever closer (13:11–14).

    B.   Rom 14:1–15:13: The "Strong" and the "Weak" should show mutual love.

        1.   Do not judge one another since Christ is the Lord and God is the Judge of us all (14:1–12).

        2.   Do not let your own conduct destroy the faith and hope of others (14:13–23).

        3.   Through steadfastness and encouragement we maintain our hope (15:1–6).

        4.   By loving one another we may all abound in hope (15:7–13).

VII. Rom 15:14–16:27: Paul relates his audience to his mission of spreading the gospel.

    A.   Paul's past apostolic success and future apostolic hope (15:14–21).

    B.   The role of the Roman Christians in Paul's future apostolate (15:22–33).

    C.   Paul greets contributors to his apostolate (16:1–16).

    D.   Final exhortation (16:17–20).

    E.   Final greetings and doxology (16:21–27).

After all of the above introductory remarks we are now ready to begin what we hope proves to be an adventurous and worthwhile reading of Paul's great Letter to the Romans.

NOTES

1. J. C. Beker, *Paul the Apostle. The Triumph of God in Life and Thought* (Philadelphia: Fortress, 1980); *Paul's Apocalyptic Gospel. The Coming Triumph of God* (Philadelphia: Fortress, 1982); W. Meeks, "Social Functions of Apocalyptic Language in Pauline Christianity," *Apocalypticism in the Mediterranean World and the Near East* (Ed. D. Hellholm; Tübingen: Mohr, 1983) 687–705.

2. S. B. Marrow, *Paul: His Letters and His Theology* (New York/Mahwah: Paulist, 1986) 5–58.

3. J. E. Stambaugh and D. L. Balch, *The New Testament in Its Social Environment* (Library of Early Christianity 2; Philadelphia: Westminster, 1986) 160–163; W. Wiefel, "The Jewish Community in Ancient Rome and the Origins of Roman Christianity," *The Romans Debate* (Ed. K. P. Donfried; Minneapolis: Augsburg, 1977) 100–119; R. Penna, "Les Juifs à Rome au temps de l'apôtre Paul," *NTS* 28 (1982) 321–347.

4. There has been considerable discussion about whether Romans 16 belongs to the original letter, but a number of recent interpreters tend to accept it. See W.-H. Ollrog, "Die Abfassungsverhältnisse von Röm 16," *Kirche* (Festschrift für G. Bornkamm zum 75. Geburtstag; ed. D. Lührmann and G. Strecker; Tübingen: Mohr, 1980) 221 n. 3, for a list of those who argue that Romans 16 belongs to Romans 1–15, to which may be added: H. Gamble, *The Textual History of the Letter to the Romans* (Studies and Documents 42; Grand Rapids: Eerdmans, 1977). We accept the conclusion of both Ollrog and Gamble that on text-critical and literary grounds Romans 16 can be fully understood as the original conclusion of the Letter to the Romans.

5. S. K. Stowers, *The Diatribe and Paul's Letter to the Romans* (SBLDS 57; Chico: Scholars Press, 1981) 175–184.

6. F. Siegert, *Argumentation bei Paulus: Gezeigt an Röm 9–11* (WUNT 34; Tübingen: Mohr, 1985) 242–247.

7. The concept of the "implied reader" of a literary text is well described by the following: R. A. Culpepper, *Anatomy of the Fourth Gospel. A Study in Literary Design* (Philadelphia: Fortress, 1983) 208–210; J. D. Kingsbury, *Matthew as Story* (Philadelphia: Fortress, 1986) 36–38.

Chapter II

Romans 1:1–17

A. Rom 1:1–7: Paul Introduces Himself and Greets the Christians at Rome.

Paul begins by boldly defining and asserting his special relationship to Jesus Christ and God as an apostle for the gospel:

1. Romans 1:1–4:

1 Paul, slave of Christ Jesus, called to be an apostle appointed for the gospel of God, 2 promised beforehand through his prophets in the holy scriptures, 3 about his Son born from David's seed (family) according to the flesh, 4 but designated Son of God with power according to the Spirit of holiness from resurrection of the dead, Jesus Christ our Lord.

a. Paul was called by God to be an apostle for the gospel.

1:1 His opening words already set the tone and establish the point of view for the Epistle which follows. Paul wants his epistolary audience to view him, first of all, as a "slave" of Christ Jesus. By relating himself to Jesus Christ as a "slave" to his "master" or "lord," Paul projects to his audience, on the one hand, a humble dependence upon and submission to the reigning power of the Lord Jesus, and on the other, the dominating authority that both constitutes and undergirds his apostleship. The epistolary audience is to perceive Paul's apostleship as a divine calling which authoritatively appointed him for the task of preaching God's gospel.

b. Paul's gospel is the promised fulfillment regarding God's Son.

1:2 In describing this gospel as the prestigious fulfillment of what God "promised beforehand through his prophets in the holy scriptures," Paul inserts it into the scriptural lineage of God's past prophetic

14

promises and thus endows it with a "promise" character of its own. As the fulfillment of God's past promises, the gospel functions as a present locus of God's salvific activity and thus awakens expectations in Paul's audience for what this gospel now means and "promises" for the future.

1:3–4 Paul's summary depiction of the gospel about God's Son is poetically constructed into two chiastically parallel verses centered around the words "with power":

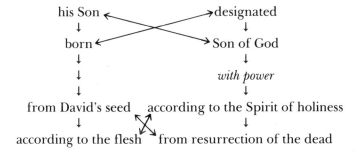

The rhetorical power of this dual expression lies in the way it heightens the audience's expectations by developing the "promise" aspect of the gospel. The first verse declares the Davidic, human heritage of Jesus, thus illustrating how the gospel fulfills God's past prophetic promises with regard to a favored son of David (e.g., 2 Sam 7:12–16; Ps 89:3–4, 20–37).

With corresponding literary elements, the second half of the expression intensifies the first by proclaiming the divine Sonship of Jesus Christ based upon his resurrection from the dead, which has established him as a Son of God equipped "*with power.*" The rhetorical emphasis clearly falls upon the words "with power," which is the only literary unit without a parallel in the first half of the expression.

Since the resurrection of Jesus begins to fulfill future eschatological expectations regarding a general resurrection of the dead, it further amplifies the "promise" nature of the gospel. And by accentuating the "power" that Jesus has gained from being raised from the dead by the force of God's Spirit and thus designated Son of God, Paul has attuned his audience's expectations toward what this "power" might mean and "promise."

By utilizing what are undoubtedly familiar, traditional, pre-Pauline terms to identify his gospel, Paul assures his Roman audience that the gospel he preaches is the same one they already know about and believe in. He is building a common bond with his audience. His succinct portrayal of the gospel's content climaxes with the words "Jesus Christ *our* Lord." Jesus Christ is the shared Lord of both Paul ("slave of Christ Jesus," 1:1) and his audience.

It is through our Lord Jesus Christ that Paul himself (or Paul and his fellow apostles and co-workers) has received a world-wide apostolate:

2. Romans 1:5–7:

5 Through whom (our Lord Jesus Christ) we have received the gift of apostleship for (the purpose of bringing about) the obedience of faith among all the peoples for the sake of his name, 6 among whom you yourselves are also called to belong to Jesus Christ. 7 To all those in Rome, beloved of God, called to be holy, grace to you and peace from God our Father and the Lord Jesus Christ!

a. Paul's apostolate is to bring all peoples to the obedience of faith.

1:5 Paul elaborates upon the goal of his divinely granted apostleship. It is not only "for" the purpose of preaching the gospel of God (1:1), but "for" the purpose of leading all peoples to obediently submit themselves in faith to the mighty lordship of Jesus Christ. This is what will promulgate "his name" as Lord and powerful Son of God. Paul has enlarged the focus of his audience toward the universal scope of his apostolate for the gospel.

b. Paul's Roman audience is included in his apostolate.

1:6–7 He then directly addresses and embraces his audience within his all-inclusive apostolate and finally extends a warm and prayerful greeting to his entire audience at Rome.

Paul has thus related himself to his epistolary audience as a divinely called, authoritative apostle for the gospel, who is now addressing the Christians at Rome because they fall within the world-wide breadth of his apostolate. He characterizes his implied audience as fellow Christians who are called to continue to belong through faith to the lordship of Jesus Christ and to continue to be "holy," separated from the ungodly realm in order to live within God's realm as God's beloved.

And he cheerfully invokes upon them the continued favor, the "grace," and the unifying, harmonious well-being, the "peace" or "shalom," that come from God, *our* common Father, and the Lord Jesus Christ. Now that he has identified, addressed and greeted his audience, Paul will speak to them more pointedly.

B. Rom: 1:8–15: Paul Has a Driving Desire to Visit and Evangelize the Romans.

Paul congratulates his audience for their world-renowned faith and thereby acknowledges their prominent position within the worldwide horizon of his apostolate:

1. Romans 1:8–10:

8 First, I thank my God through Jesus Christ concerning all of you, for your faith is proclaimed in all the world. 9 For God is my witness, whom I serve with my spirit in the gospel of his Son, how ceaselessly I make mention of you 10 always in my prayers, begging that somehow, sometime, at last I may succeed by God's will to come to you.

a. *The faith of the Romans is known throughout the world.*

1:8 By so complimenting the Romans, Paul draws them closer to himself and to his apostolic point of view, as he makes their faith a matter of his personal thanksgiving to "my God through Jesus Christ." That the Romans already possess the faith which is the primary goal of Paul's apostolate and that this faith is well-known throughout the world not only gratifies Paul and his God, but automatically incorporates them into Paul's God-given, world-wide apostolate. In other words, Paul has broadened the vision of his audience by relating their faith to God and to the rest of the world.

b. *Paul has long prayed to visit the Romans.*

1:9–10 Continuing to speak from the purview of God's plan, Paul divulges to his audience how earnestly he has desired to visit them. Paul is building a closer and closer bond with his audience. As he impresses upon them how he is totally governed by God's will in his preaching of the gospel, he establishes his long-standing, deep yearning to visit them. Even this visit to Rome is a matter of God's will and of Paul's personal prayer as apostle. His audience is to be duly struck by how important they are to Paul and his apostolate and by how sincerely he wishes to come to them.

But why is Paul so interested in visiting the Romans? Because such a visitation would be mutually beneficial:

we don't often anticipate being encouraged by a strange congregation

2. *Romans 1:11–15:*

11 For I long to see you, so that I may impart to you some spiritual gift to strengthen you, 12 that is, to be mutually encouraged along with you through each other's faith, both yours and mine. 13 I should like you to know, brothers, that I have often intended to come to you— but I have been prevented even until now—so that I may have some results among you as well as among the rest of the peoples. 14 I am under obligation to both Greeks and barbarians, to both the wise and the unlearned: 15 so I am eager to preach the gospel also to you who are in Rome.

a. *Paul's desire to encourage and strengthen his audience.*

1:11–12 This titillates the curiosity of the audience. What is this indefinite "spiritual gift" with which Paul wants to strengthen them? How can the faith of Paul "encourage" them, and moreover, how can their faith "encourage" him? In this process of arousing his audience's anticipations, Paul emphasizes his common bond with them through the faith they share. It is "each other's faith, *both yours and mine*," that can mutually encourage Paul and the Romans.

b. *Paul has been detained from evangelizing at Rome.*

1:13 The affinity Paul is establishing with his audience becomes more intimate as he refers to them as his "brothers." The words "I should like you to know" are literally a double negative expression— "I do not want you to be ignorant," which very forcefully calls for the audience's special attention to what Paul is disclosing to them.

By informing them that he had already on many occasions determined to visit them, Paul reinforces his previously stated desire to come to Rome and continues to instill in his audience how vitally important they are to him and his apostolate.

Unfortunately, Paul was prevented (by God, "divine passive") from realizing his previous intentions and, moreover, he is still prevented "even until now" from visiting them. This sets the stage for the Letter itself to serve as a substitute for Paul's personal presence at Rome. It strongly implies that it is in and through the Epistle itself that Paul intends to accomplish his purpose of spiritually strengthening and encouraging the faith that the Roman Christians already possess.

The "results" (literally, "fruit") that Paul hopes to effect through his visit would be those that God himself would work through Paul's preaching of the gospel at Rome, whether that would mean non-believers coming to the "obedience of faith" (1:5) or believers being strengthened and encouraged in their faith. At any rate, Paul has once again related his audience to "the rest of the peoples" and thereby included them within the domain of his apostolate for the gospel.

c. So Paul will now present his gospel in the Letter.

1:14–15 Since Paul has been commissioned to bring the gospel to all peoples, regardless of social status, he is anxious to evangelize those in Rome. Although Paul cannot yet journey to Rome, he can and will present his gospel to his fellow Roman Christians, now, in the Letter to follow.

C. Rom 1:16–17: Paul Announces the Gospel of God's Power.

And so Paul begins anew by assertively introducing and defining for his audience his own rendition of the gospel:

1. Romans 1:16:

16 For I am not ashamed of the gospel: it is the power of God for salvation to all who believe, to Jew first but also to Greek.

a. The gospel does not "shame" Paul.

1:16 In candidly confessing his deep confidence of not being "ashamed" of preaching the gospel, that is, of not being forsakenly "shamed" before or by God either presently or in the final judgment, Paul already displays an attitude of hope meant to begin to spiritually strengthen and encourage his auditors. They are to be encouraged by their faith in the same gospel of which Paul is openly and publicly "not ashamed." They likewise need and should not be "ashamed" of their adherence to the gospel.

b. The gospel is the power of God for the salvation of all.

Paul's listeners can be encouraged by their faith in the gospel because the gospel itself is the very "power of God" which leads to and assures the salvation of all who believe in it. It was offered first to Jews because of their privileged place in God's plan of salvation, but it is now also available to Greeks and thus to the totality of humankind.

By defining the gospel as the "*power*" of God, Paul links his own recapitulation of the gospel to the previous, more traditional summary which emphatically stressed and instilled in the mind of his audience the "*power*" now operative in the gospel about God's Son (1:3–4). This "power of God" which is the gospel thus constitutes for Paul's audience and all who believe a source of strength and hope for their ultimate salvation.

2. Romans 1:17:

17 For the righteousness of God is revealed in it from faith to faith, as it is written, "He who is righteous from faith will live" (Hab 2:4).

a. The "righteousness of God" is now revealed in the gospel.

1:17 The gospel operates as the salvific power of God because the "righteousness of God" has now been finally and definitively "revealed" within it. The word "righteousness" attempts to render into English the rich and rather difficult to translate Greek biblical concept of *dikaiosyne*. It is a relational concept referring to the appropriate mode of action or behavior that should prevail among the parties who are united by a certain relationship.

In the biblical tradition God and his chosen people have been bonded together in a covenantal relationship requiring mutual fidelity. God is to be their true and faithful God; they are to be God's true and faithful people, as concretely manifested both toward God and toward one another, by their careful and faithful observance of God's covenantal commandments. In succumbing, however, to the overwhelming power and domination of sinfulness, God's people unfortunately could not uphold or remain faithful to their part of the relationship—their "righteousness" or "faithfulness" failed. Fortunately and wonderfully, God has taken it upon himself to uphold both ends of the relationship with his people. This is what is meant by the "righteousness of *God*"—God's very own "righteousness" or "faithfulness," both to himself as God and to his created and chosen people, which "justifies" or "rectifies" the ruptured relationship with his people. Perhaps, then, it would be better to translate *dikaiosyne theou* as God's "rectifying faithfulness" or his "justifying fidelity."

b. The "righteousness of God" is appropriated by faith.

Keeping in mind the apocalyptic-eschatological framework of Paul's thought, this previously unknown and unheard of, hidden "righteousness of God" has now been plainly, publicly, positively and decisively "revealed" or "manifested" within God's gospel of power. God's righteousness or rectifying faithfulness has now been revealed in the gospel within the dimension of "faith"—"from faith to faith." This marvelous righteousness of God, his justifying fidelity, is accepted, submitted to, or appropriated simply by believing, by placing one's obediential trust in this new salvific activity of God. Its reception begins and ends with faith.

c. Believing in the "righteousness of God" means "life".

Now that this righteousness of God has been distinctly revealed in the gospel about his Son, the ancient prophetic promise as recorded in God's holy scriptures from Habakkuk 2:4 has reached its end-time fulfillment. The person who has now been made "just" or "righteous" by accepting the righteousness of God through faith "will live."

This quotation has a double meaning based on the grammatical "double-duty" of the prepositional phrase "from faith." It means both that the person who is "made righteous from faith" *will live,* and that the person who is made righteous will now "*live* from faith." The righteous person is both made righteous from faith and now "lives" from this rectifying faith. The "life" that the righteous or just person "will live" refers to the future, eschatological life with God that the believer may now, already, begin to live within the realm of faith.

d. Paul begins to encourage and strengthen his readers with the hope for "salvation" and "life."

Paul is beginning to awaken in his audience the responses of encouragement and spiritual strength that they may share with him based upon their common Christian faith (1:11–12). The implied audience has been aroused to confidently hope, like Paul, for the *salvation* to be effected by the power of God which is the gospel and for the gift of God's end-time, eternal *life.*

Paul has skillfully positioned his Roman audience toward his point of view and into certain significant relationships: he has related his implied readers to the gospel of God/Jesus Christ; he has drawn his readers as fellow Christians very closely to himself; and he has related them to the rest of the world, thus situating them within the world-wide domain of his apostolate. Having announced his gospel as the theme of the Letter, Paul has prepared his epistolary audience for the fuller explanation of his gospel which now follows. He has indicated that "spiritual strength" and "encouragement" are the major responses he wishes to effect in his implied audience. And so now we want to see how Paul's presentation of the gospel in the rest of the Letter will accomplish this.

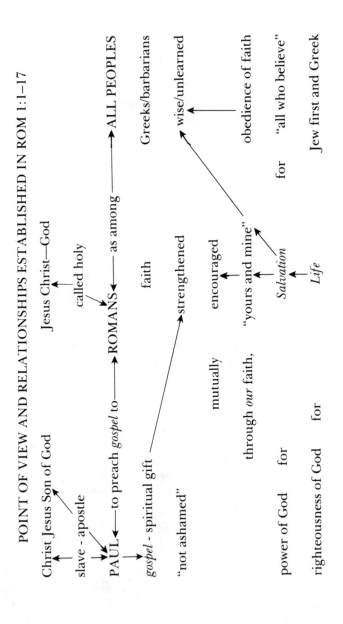

POINT OF VIEW AND RELATIONSHIPS ESTABLISHED IN ROM 1:1–17

Christ Jesus Son of God

Jesus Christ—God

slave - apostle

called holy

PAUL ——to preach *gospel* to——→ ROMANS ——— as among ——→ ALL PEOPLES

gospel - spiritual gift

faith   Greeks/barbarians

"not ashamed"   strengthened   wise/unlearned

mutually   encouraged

through *our* faith,   "yours and mine"   obedience of faith

Salvation

power of God   for   for   "all who believe"

righteousness of God   for   *Life*   Jew first and Greek

Chapter III

Romans 1:18–3:20

A. Rom 1:18–32: Paul Disgusts His Audience with the Behavior of the "Ungodly."

After uplifting his readers with his initial announcement of the gospel, Paul suddenly shifts gears and alters the tone. The hope-filled proclamation of the gospel of God's power leading to universally coveted "salvation" and of the revelation of God's rectifying faithfulness meaning a new "life" with God for all who believe (1:16–17) is followed by a discouraging declaration evoking disgust in his implied readership. In correlative contrast to the decisive "righteousness" of God which has now been "revealed" in the gospel, the definitive "wrath" or "anger" of God has now become painfully evident:

1. Romans 1:18–23:

18 For the wrath of God is revealed from heaven upon all ungodliness and unrighteousness of persons who suppress the truth by unrighteousness. 19 For what can be known about God is clear to them, because God himself has made it clear to them. 20 For his invisible attributes, namely, his eternal power and deity, are visible from the creation of the world, perceived in the things that have been made, so that they are without excuse. 21 For although they knew God they did not honor him as God or give thanks to him, but they were made futile in their thoughts and their senseless minds were darkened. 22 Alleging to be wise, they have become foolish 23 and exchanged the glory of the immortal God for a likeness, an image of mortal man or of birds, animals or reptiles.

a. The "wrath of God" is now evident in all ungodly behavior.

1:18 The "wrath of God" (*orge theou*) is the negative obverse of the "righteousness of God"; it is the form that the righteousness of God assumes against ungodliness, wickedness or unrighteousness. Although the "wrath of God" had always been experienced in one way or another throughout history, in the apocalyptic-eschatological mentality it was expected to be fully manifested as ultimate punishment and condemnation on the day of God's final judgment (see Rom 2:5, 8). Paul is asserting that this "wrath of God" is now "revealed" from heaven with a new, final, end-time and decisive quality, as is already evident in the unrighteous behavior of the ungodly, who suppress God's "truth," his fidelity, toward his creatures.

b. God has permitted the ungodly to be victims of their own idolatrous perversions.

1:19–21 These misguided "ungodly" are fully responsible and deserving of God's wrath. It is not as if they could not recognize God. Nevertheless, the "ungodly" have refused to properly acknowledge God and thus have experienced the "wrath of God" in their perverted way of thinking. God's wrath and appropriate retribution is beginning to emerge here with the implication that God himself has allowed the ungodly to become victims of their own futile and senseless mentality.

1:22–23 With pathetic irony Paul brings their amazing and almost comical stupidity to the fore: Although the ungodly want to be and suppose that they are "wise," they are actually quite "foolish." They have ridiculously chosen to worship and serve a mere "likeness, an image" (doubly expressed for emphasis) over "glory"; they have astoundingly opted for what is "mortal" instead of what is "immortal"; and although his power and deity is clearly apparent in and through his creation, they have incredibly mistaken the Creator "God" for his creatures—mere human beings and animals:

Ironical Opposites in Rom 1:22–23

"foolish" instead of "wise"
"likeness, image" instead of "glory"
"mortal" instead of "immortal"
"creatures" instead of "Creator"

This poignantly illustrates the "unrighteousness" or "unfaithfulness" of the ungodly toward the Creator and his, as well as their fellow, creatures. In totally misconstruing the divinely intended right and proper relations that should exist among Creator and creatures (see Gen 1:24–31; Deut 4:15–19), the ungodly effectively obstruct and prevent the Creator's "truth" or "faithfulness" from prevailing (1:18). And so Paul derides the idolatrous practices prevalent among the multiplicity of religious cults in the Roman empire.[1] He is persuading his audience to look upon the plight of these ungodly with pity and repulsion.

The revelation of God's wrath and the perversion of the divine order of creation is also apparent in the behavior of the ungodly toward themselves:

2. Romans 1:24–27:

24 Therefore God gave them up in the lusts of their hearts to impurity, to degrading their bodies among themselves, 25 those who exchanged the truth about God for a lie and worshiped and served the creature instead of the Creator, who is blessed forever! Amen. 26 For this reason God gave them up to disgraceful passions. Their women exchanged natural sexual relations for unnatural, 27 and likewise the men, abandoning natural sexual relations with women, were consumed with passion for one another—men committing indecent acts with men and receiving in their own persons the inevitable recompense for their perversion.

a. God has given the ungodly over to unnatural degradations of themselves.

1:24–25 The wrath of God upon the ungodly is manifest here in God's simply "giving them up" or "handing them over" to the evil of their own ways. Vice is its own punishment. God allows the ungodly the freedom of degrading themselves and distorting their proper relationship both toward the Creator and his creatures.

Paul's spontaneous outburst of praise for the Creator exemplifies the correct reverence befitting God and safeguards himself and his audience from the incorrect reverence of the ungodly.

b. The ungodly do not respect the proper distinction and complementarity between the sexes.

1:26–27 God's wrath upon the ungodly is further manifested in his giving them over to their lesbian and homosexual activity. Such deviate practices disturb the divinely willed distinction and complementarity that is to exist between the sexes (Gen 1:27; Lev 18:22; 20:13).[2]

This further demonstrates the "unrighteousness" or "unfaithfulness" of the ungodly toward the Creator and his creatures and continues the call for the disgust and aversion of the reader.

Paul goes on to graphically illumine the thoroughly depraved mentality and degenerate conduct of the ungodly:

3. Romans 1:28–32:

28 And as they did not think it fit to acknowledge God, God gave them up to an unfit mind, to do improper things. 29 They were filled with every kind of unrighteousness, wickedness, greediness, malice; full of envy, murder, rivalry, deceit, malignity, they are gossips, 30 slanderers, God haters, insolent, arrogant, boastful, inventors of evil, disobedient to parents, 31 senseless, faithless, heartless, merciless. 32 Although they know perfectly well God's decree that those who do such things are worthy of death, they not only do them but they even approve those who do them!

a. God has given the ungodly over to every manner of unfitting conduct.

1:28 With a clever play on words ("think it fit," *edokimasan*/"unfit," *adokimon*) Paul ties together the two parts of another blunt expression of God's adequate retribution toward the ungodly. In appropriate correspondence to their decision not to respect God, God suitably counters by "giving them up" to the folly of their decision and lets them be the victims of their own unfitting behavior.

1:29–31 Paul vividly describes their unfitting behavior by attributing to them a staggering list of vices. The list has an unmistakably powerful rhetorical effect. It begins with the first four vices linked in literary assonance and builds to an emphatic conclusion in which the last four vices are adjoined in artistic alliteration:

> asynetous—asynthetous—astorgous—aneleemonas
> senseless—faithless—heartless—merciless

The variety and mere accumulation of these undesirable traits relentlessly bombards and overwhelms the reader with the utter and thorough degradation of the ungodly.

b. The ungodly endorse the death-bringing wickedness of themselves and others.

1:32 Paul affixes a climax to his depiction of the ungodly, which intensifies their appalling condition to the extreme. Being fully cognizant of the right relationships and way of living God wants and justly demands, the ungodly are fully responsible for their deplorable position. Even the awareness that their wayward conduct rightly deserves and will inevitably lead to a penalty of death does not deter them. Despite this destiny of death, the ungodly not only continue their sinister patterns but even go so far as to approve of others who descend to their abysmal level and follow in their footsteps. Certainly Paul and his readers must strongly and repulsively disapprove and thoroughly condemn such conduct.

Paul could hardly paint a more depressing and bleak picture of the utter despair of this "ungodly," "unrighteous" group of people upon whom the dreaded "wrath of God" is clearly evident. In the process of leading his audience through a compelling consideration of the desperate plight of these damned "ungodly," Paul has effectively evoked the disapproval, disgust, repugnance and revulsion of his audience toward them. The why and wherefore of this remains to be seen.

B. Rom 2:1–16: Paul Confronts His Audience as among the Morally "Upright."

After firmly anchoring his audience into a standpoint of judgment and condemnation against the ungodly, Paul suddenly pulls the rug out from under their feet:

1. Romans 2:1–4:

1 Therefore you are without excuse, each and everyone of you who judges, for in judging another you condemn yourself, because you who judge do the very same things! 2 We know that the judgment of God rightly falls upon those who do such things. 3 Do you suppose, O you who judge those who do such things and yet do them yourself, that you will escape the judgment of God? 4 Or do you think lightly of the wealth of his kindness and tolerance and patience, unaware that the kindness of God is meant to lead you to repentance?

a. Paul's judgmental readers are as inexcusable as the ungodly.

2:1 This is the first instance of Paul's use of the diatribal manner of argumentation, in which he indicts an imaginary interlocutor.

Through this device of direct dialogue with an imaginary auditor Paul indirectly addresses his implied audience, who readily identify with the imaginary figure.

Although Paul's audience has been rightly led to strongly abhor and condemn the conduct of the ungodly, Paul embarrasses them with the same charge he had levelled earlier against the ungodly—they are "without excuse" before God (see 1:19). In fact, the audience, who were just forced to pass judgment upon the ungodly, are now constrained to condemn themselves, since they do the very things which they justly condemn others for doing. Although they are able to condemn evil as evil, they are unable to avoid it. Paul has adroitly entrapped and entangled them in a predicament of their own.

b. Those who judge evil yet still do it are liable to God's condemnation.

2:2 It must be commonly accepted by Paul and his audience that since they do the same things the ungodly do, they deserve the same judgment from God.

2:3 In the diatribal manner of interrogation Paul continues to ensnare his auditors. The ability merely to judge wrongdoing as wrong, but not being able to avoid that same wrongdoing, will not win one's acquittal before the judgment seat of God.

2:4 Paul's auditors should not be misled by or presume upon God's present stance of generous kindness, tolerance and patience toward their own wrongdoing. They should know that God is simply giving them a chance and waiting for them to turn from their wicked ways.

Unfortunately Paul's implied audience is not presently paying proper heed to God's kind forbearance:

2. Romans 2:5–8:

5 For in accord with your stubbornness and unrepentant heart you are storing up for yourself wrath for the day of wrath and revelation of the just judgment of God, 6 who will repay each according to his deeds. 7 To those who by perseverance of good deeds seek glory and honor and immortality, (God will give) eternal life; 8 but for those who are selfish and disobey the truth while obeying unrighteousness, there will be wrath and rage.

a. *Those who remain stubbornly unrepentant will receive the wrath of God in the last judgment.*

2:5 Although the "wrath of God" is not presently visible in the lives of Paul's listeners as it already is in the conduct of those who are clearly "ungodly" (1:18–32), it is merely being postponed. In accord with Paul's apocalyptic-eschatological outlook, God's terrible wrath will appear with full fury on the day of God's just judgment of those in Paul's audience who obdurately refuse to take advantage of God's enduring patience and turn from their evil ways.

b. *In the judgment God will repay each person strictly in accord with his/her good or evil deeds.*

2:6 On that day God will judge and repay each human being on the basis of his/her actual "deeds," not on the basis, then, of one's judgment against evil or of one's intentions to do good.

2:7–8 As Paul unambiguously states it, God will appropriately reward each person strictly according to his/her actual conduct. Those who consistently perform good acts will inherit God's eternal life, while those who persist in selfishness and disobedience of God are destined for God's fierce and furious wrath.

And so Paul sounds a note of caution and alarm in the ears of his audience, lest they think they will fare any better in the judgment than the "ungodly" whom they rightly condemn.

Neither can Paul's audience expect or rely upon any kind of exception or special preference on God's part toward them in the judgment:

3. Romans 2:9–13:

9 There will be affliction and anguish upon every human being who does evil, Jew first and also Greek, 10 but glory and honor and peace for everyone who does good, Jew first and also Greek. 11 For there is no partiality from God. 12 Those who have sinned outside the Law will also perish outside the Law, and those who have sinned under the Law will be judged by the Law. 13 For it is not the hearers of the Law who are righteous before God, but it is the doers of the Law who will be pronounced righteous.

a. *God will reward all who do good and punish all who do evil without exception.*

2:9–10 All without exception will be punished if they do evil and rewarded if they do good. And the totality of humankind will be so judged—the Jews first because of their God-given preeminent role in salvation history, but then also the Greeks and thus all of humanity, whether Jew or Greek.

2:11 No one will escape judgment according to works, for God makes no exceptions and grants no special favors to one group over another when it comes to judgment.

b. Those who hear the Law yet still sin will be condemned by God.

2:12 Naturally those who have sinned outside the realm or domain of the Law will simply perish without the Law. But even those who have sinned within the domain of the Law can anticipate and count on no special status in the judgment simply because they lived under the realm of the Law, for they will be strictly judged by that Law.

2:13 Furthermore, those who merely listen to what the Law commands without practicing it have no hope of being declared "righteous" or "just" by God in the judgment according to one's deeds.

And so Paul persists in persuading his audience against fostering any ideas that they might receive some sort of favored treatment from God in the judgment because they may appear and think themselves to be morally upright and can distinguish themselves from the corrupt "ungodly."

Paul finally undermines any notion that the mere external possession of the Law might count for something in the judgment:

4. Romans 2:14–16:

14 Whenever Gentiles who do not have the Law by nature do the requirements of the Law, they become a "Law" to themselves, even though they do not have the Law. 15 They show that what the Law requires is written in their hearts, while their conscience also bears witness and their conflicting reasonings accuse or perhaps excuse them 16 on the day when, according to my gospel, God judges the secrets of human beings by Christ Jesus.

a. Those who do not possess the Law may still observe it from the heart.

2:14–15 Just as merely having listened to the Law, so merely having possessed the Law externally means nothing before God in the judgment. What is important is the faithful observance and practice of the Law. And this is possible even for those who have not been given the Law externally. For example, Gentiles who have not been given the Law by nature and yet do what the Law commands demonstrate that the Law can be observed internally, from the heart, even when it is not possessed externally.

b. God will judge the hidden secrets of the human heart.

2:15–16 And it is this internal observance of what the Law requires that will be the basis of judgment. For through Christ Jesus God will judge the interior secrets of the human heart, according to Paul's gospel. Consequently, those who by nature possess the Law externally must also practice it internally and sincerely from the heart.

Paul thus eliminates from his audience's mind any thoughts of partiality before God for merely possessing the Law without doing it.

C. Rom 2:17–3:8: Paul Startles His Audience with a Critique of the "Upright" Jew.

Paul then centers in on commonly accepted notions regarding a privileged position before God for those who are Jewish:

1. Romans 2:17–20:

17 If you call yourself a Jew and rely upon the Law and boast in God 18 and know his will and discern what is important, because you are instructed in the Law, 19 and if you are convinced that you are a guide to the blind, a light to those in darkness, 20 an instructor of the foolish, a teacher of children, because you have in the Law the embodiment of knowledge and truth.

a. Jews are privileged to have the Law and know the will of God.

2:17 Here Paul reverts to the diatribal device of indirectly addressing his audience by directly confronting an imaginary and representative "Jew." In this summary description Paul plays upon the legitimate pride of being Jewish. It is an honored privilege just to be able to call oneself "Jew," because Jews can "rely" upon their special gift of God's Law, which enables them to "boast," that is, have a bold and delightfully deep confidence, in God himself.

2:18 Graciously permitted to know God's will and to be educated in his Law, they are enabled to determine what is important to God.

b. Jews have the prerogative and responsibility of teaching others the ways of God.

2:19–20 They are thus equipped and called to lead people to God's ways, to instruct the foolish and to teach children the wisdom of

a way of life in accord with God's will, because they are the ones chosen
to possess the great gift of God's Law, the actual, concrete embodiment
of divine knowledge and truth.

But unfortunately the Jews have not lived up to their privileged
responsibilities. With a rapid salvo of piercingly incriminating questions Paul lowers the boom on them:

2. Romans 2:21–24:

21 You then who teach others, do you teach yourself? You who
preach 'Do not steal', do you steal? 22 You who say 'Do not commit
adultery', do you commit adultery? You who abhor idols, do you rob
temples? 23 You who boast in the Law, do you dishonor God through
transgression of the Law? 24 For, as is written, "The name of God is
blasphemed among the Gentiles because of you." (Isa 52:5)

a. The Jews have miserably failed to live up to their God-given privilege and responsibility.

2:21–23 The Jews have not practiced the very commandments of
the Law that they have been entrusted by God to preach! They have
miserably failed to keep the very Law in which they so proudly "boast."
Rather than honoring God by carrying out their special responsibility
of instructing others in the will of God, they have shamefully dishon-
ored God by transgressing his Law.

b. The Jews have brought dishonor to God among the Gentiles.

2:24 Moreover, instead of promoting and advancing God's glorious name among the Gentiles by being exemplary models of the Law
they supposedly cherish and by being "guides" and "lights" who lead
the Gentiles to God, they have actually ignominiously fulfilled the prophetic text of Isaiah 52:5 by causing the name of God to be "blasphemed," not honored, among the Gentiles.

Paul is forcing his audience to dismiss any previously held beliefs
that the Jews will be favored in God's judgment because they possess
and know his Law.

Neither will the external sign of circumcision afford the Jews any
advantage in God's final judgment:

3. Romans 2:25–29:

25 Circumcision indeed is of value if you practice the Law; but if
you are a transgressor of the Law, your circumcision has become un-

circumcision. 26 So, if one who is uncircumcised keeps the precepts of the Law, will not his uncircumcision be counted as circumcision? 27 Then those who are physically uncircumcised yet observe the Law will judge you who for all your written code and circumcision are nevertheless a transgressor of the Law. 28 For he is not a real Jew who is one outwardly, nor is true circumcision an external and physical matter. 29 But he is a real Jew who is one inwardly, and true circumcision is a matter of the heart, inspired by the spirit not by the letter (of the Law). His praise is not from men but from God.

a. The uncircumcised who do the Law will judge the Jews who transgress it.

2:25 Jewish failure to faithfully obey the Law has rendered their special sign of circumcision, which would distinguish them from others in the judgment, the same as uncircumcision.

2:26–27 In fact, the tables will be turned on the Jews in the judgment. Astoundingly, the uncircumcised, whose uncircumcision God will count the same as circumcision in the judgment if they keep the Law, will actually sit in judgment over the Jews who break the Law despite having its written code and the physical sign of circumcision! Not Law-possessing, circumcised Jews but Law-abiding, uncircumcised Gentiles will have the position of honor in the judgment!

b. The true Jew has a heart inspired by the spirit of God's Law.

2:28 What is more, even the name "Jew" and the Jewish mark of "circumcision" need to be redefined. Neither physical externals nor outward, public appearance defines the genuine Jew and true circumcision.

2:29 The real Jew is the one who lives sincerely and inwardly from the true circumcision of the heart. He faithfully obeys God's Law by being true to the interior inspiration of the spirit, not by being concerned about keeping the letter of the Law for appearance's sake. He strives for and wins the bona fide praise of God rather than the empty adulation of human beings.

Paul has stunned his audience with this penetrating attack which disintegrates commonly held ideas about a distinctive position for Jews in God's judgment.

But if this is the case, what about the renowned election of the Jews as God's chosen people in salvation history? Do they really have a unique role to play in God's plan? As Paul in diatribal style queries:

4. Romans 3:1–4:

1 Then what advantage has the Jew? Or what is the benefit of circumcision? 2 Much in every way! In the first place, they have been entrusted with the promises of God. 3 What if some have been unfaithful? Surely their faithlessness will not nullify the faithfulness of God? 4 By no means! God must remain true, even if every human being is false, as is written, "That you may be vindicated by your promises, and be victorious when you are tried." (Ps 51:4)

a. The Jews have been entrusted with God's powerful promises.

3:1–2 Although the Jews cannot rely upon their Jewishness, possession of the Law or circumcision to carry them through the last judgment, they still have an important place in God's salvific design. As well documented throughout the scriptures, God has entrusted the Jewish people with his powerful promises. It is through them that God has chosen to work out and fulfill his promises for salvation.

b. The unfaithfulness of the Jews cannot obstruct God's faithfulness.

3:3 Even if they have been unfaithful to their part of the covenantal relationship with God, this will not prevent God from carrying out his salvific promises through them.

3:4 In fact, he will remain totally faithful to his promises toward his people and humankind, even if there is no human being faithful to him. As the scriptures (Ps 51:4) testify, the complete fulfillment of God's promises will demonstrate and vindicate his faithfulness to himself, his people and his creation. No one will be able to successfully indict him, since the achievement of his words of salvation will win his triumph over any accusations.

But neither the Jews nor anyone else in Paul's audience should attempt to misinterpret and distort this marvelously abiding fidelity of God by pervertedly glorying in their own shortcomings. As part of his lively, diatribal manner of argumentation Paul begins by speaking in the first person plural to characterize a collective stance:

5. Romans 3:5–8:

5 But if our lack of uprightness serves to show forth God's righteousness, what shall we say? Surely not that God is unjust to bring

down wrath?—(I am speaking from the human point of view.) 6 By no means! Otherwise, how is God to judge the world? 7 But if through my refusal of the truth the truthfulness of God abounds to his glory, then why am I still being condemned as a sinner? 8 But surely we are not to do evil so that good may come?—as we are libelled and as some even affirm that we say. Their condemnation is deserved!

a. Provoking the just wrath of God will not benefit the sinner.

3:5–7 Here Paul rhetorically presents a perverted bit of reasoning to be ridiculed and rejected by his audience. It erroneously seeks to make the provocation of the wrath of God actually work in favor of the sinner. In other words, if human unfaithfulness ultimately results in God's faithfulness and righteousness shining forth all the more brightly, even if in the form of God justly and rightly unleashing the furor of his wrath in judgment, then why should anyone be condemned for being a sinner, since sin, in the long run, actually seems to bring about the greater glory of God?

b. Paul does not advocate the doing of evil to bring about good.

3:8 But this is an absurd, ludicrous and twisted misrepresentation of the proper relationship that is to prevail between God and his people. It would open the way for the preposterous principle that we may do evil so that good may result, which apparently Paul has been falsely accused of advocating. The condemnation of such opponents is fully deserved in a double sense—they are justly condemned for wrongly slandering Paul's position and they are still to be rightly condemned as sinners, despite the feeble and futile attempt to reason otherwise.

Paul has swayed his audience against such an inane and warped way of viewing the triumph of divine faithfulness over human infidelity.

D. Rom 3:9–20: Paul Entraps His Audience among All Who Are Sinners.

As Paul has been convincingly demonstrating and now decisively asserts, there will be no advantage or preference in God's judgment for Jews or anyone else:

1. Romans 3:9–18:

9 What then? Are we (Jews) any better off? No, not at all! For we have already accused all, Jews as well as Greeks, of being under the power of sin, 10 as it is written:

> "None is righteous, no, not one;
> 11   Not one understands;
>   Not one seeks for God.
> 12   All have turned aside, together they have become depraved;
>   Not one does good, no, not even so much as one (Ps 14:1–3).
> 13   Their throat is an opened grave;
>   With their tongues they deceive (Ps 5:9);
>   The poison of asps is under their lips (Ps 140:3);
> 14   Their mouth is filled with cursing and bitterness (Ps 10:7).
> 15   Swift are their feet to shed blood;
> 16   Ruin and misery are in their paths;
> 17   But the path of peace they do not know (Isa 59:7–8).
> 18   There is no reverence of God before their eyes" (Ps 36:1).

a. All of humanity is entangled within the power of sinfulness.

3:9 Paul has arrived at his climactic point that all of humanity, from those obviously "ungodly" to those supposedly "upright," whether Jews or Greeks, are hopelessly entrenched under the utterly corrupting power of sin.

b. Absolutely no human being lives in proper respect of God.

3:10–12 He deftly employs a rhetorically powerful and vividly poetic mosaic of scriptural quotes to forcefully drive home this point to his audience. Through a pointedly pulsating repetition of the negative terms, "none/no/not one," Paul inundates his readers with the absolutely exceptionless universality of those who are sinners. The apex is that there exists "not even so much as one" human being who is not a sinner.

3:13–14 By highlighting certain parts of the vocal organs (throat/tongues/lips/mouth) Paul colorfully emphasizes the lethally corrupting effects (opened grave/deceive/poison/cursing and bitterness) of sinful speech.

3:15–17 In the biblical tradition the concept of "way" or "path" often characterizes one's conduct or way of life. Paul poetically utilizes terms associated with "way" or "path" (feet/paths/path) to poignantly depict the deadly and destructive results (shed blood/ruin and misery/peace they do not know) of the way of sinfulness.

3:18 In completing the list of bodily members (throat/tongues/lips/mouth/feet/eyes) taken over by the decadent power of sin and returning to the negative term, "there is not," the last line succinctly sums up the whole—there is simply no reverence, respect or fear of God before the eyes of human beings.

With the authoritative aid of God's holy scriptures, then, Paul has successfully indicted all of humanity, including his audience, as sinners.

The Law is no help to this situation of universal sinfulness. Indeed, it is the Law which holds all accountable to God and ultimately causes all to experience the power of sin:

2. *Romans 3:19–20:*

19 We know that whatever the Law says it speaks to those who are under the Law, so that every mouth may be stopped and the whole world may be held accountable to God. 20 Because no human being will be justified in his sight by works of Law, for through Law comes merely consciousness of sin.

a. *The Law holds all of sinful humanity accountable to God.*

3:19 It is the common knowledge of Paul and his audience ("we know") that the commandments of God's Law apply to those who come under its jurisdiction, namely all of humanity. Consequently, there is no one who can present a legitimate defense, "every mouth is stopped," for not doing what the Law says. It is the Law itself which holds the whole world accountable to God for transgressing it and failing to perform the works or deeds it requires of all.

b. *The Law brings experience of sin rather than justification.*

3:20 And so, in the final judgment not one human being will be justified or pronounced "righteous" before God for having accomplished the works of the Law. Unfortunately, since no one does the Law, all the Law can manage to do is cause everyone to experience the full effects of the power of sinfulness.

With his emphasis on the universal (every mouth/whole world/no human being) failure to observe the Law, Paul has enclosed and tightly locked his audience within the utter hopelessness of universal sinfulness—all of humanity without exception are under the devastating power of sin.

E. Summary

Paul first persuaded his readers to react with a thoroughly abhor-ring disgust toward those who live a blatantly "ungodly" lifestyle (1:18–32). But then he surprised and embarrassed his audience by un-masking their own faults and failures, despite their ability to disap-prove of "ungodliness" and despite their apparent moral uprightness (2:1–16).

He astounded his audience by eliminating generally accepted no-tions about a special status and prerogatives for the Jews as God's cho-sen people. He has thus added to the despair of his audience by impressing upon them that if the Jews have no hope of a favored po-sition in God's last judgment, then no one has (2:17–3:8).

Finally, Paul climactically intensified the hopelessness of his au-dience by situating them squarely within the domain of universal sin-fulness (3:9–20). Paul has levelled and lowered his implied readers down to the deepest depths of despair by rhetorically inducing them to react toward and identify with various groups in a dramatically pro-gressive fashion:

The Sinful Groups in Romans 1:18–3:20

The Totally Unrighteous, Ungodly (1:18–32)

The Supposedly Morally Upright (2:1–16)

The Supposedly Upright Jew (2:17–3:8)

All Sinners (3:9–20) including Paul's READERS

Must all these sinners and Paul's audience simply resign them-selves to this utter hopelessness, or is there hope for those so shackled by the chains of this bleak and morbid despair?

NOTES

1. Stambaugh and Balch, *Social Environment*, 127–137; H. Koester, *In-troduction to the New Testament: Volume One: History, Culture, and Religion of the Hellenistic Age* (Philadelphia: Fortress, 1982) 153–204.

2. V. P. Furnish, "Homosexuality," *Harper's Bible Dictionary* (ed. P. J. Ach-temeier; San Francisco: Harper & Row, 1985) 402: "The prevailing model for homosexuality in Paul's day involved the sexual exploitation of a preadoles-cent youth by an adult male for the purposes of the adult's own gratification.

This practice was widely condemned by the apostle's non-Christian contemporaries, often with remarks similar to his in Rom. 1:26–27, where it is likely that the same kind of practice is in mind." See also M. H. Pope, "Homosexuality," *The Interpreter's Dictionary of the Bible Supplementary Volume* (Nashville: Abingdon, 1976) 415–417.

Chapter IV

Romans 3:21–4:25

A. Rom 3:21–31: All Are Now Graciously Justified by God Apart from the Law.

Having enshrouded and entombed his audience within a dark pessimism of gloom and doom, Paul immediately begins to revive their hope with an exuberant and encouraging proclamation:

1. *Romans 3:21–26:*

21 But now, apart from the Law, the righteousness of God has been manifested, attested by the Law and the Prophets, 22 the righteousness of God through faith in Jesus Christ for all who believe. For there is no distinction; 23 all have sinned and fall short of the glory of God, 24 but are freely justified by his grace through the redemption which is in Christ Jesus, 25 whom God publicly put forward as an expiation by his own blood, appropriated through faith, to be a demonstration of his righteousness through the passing over of past sins 26 in God's forbearance, for the same demonstration of his righteousness in the present time, in order to show that he is just and justifies anyone who has faith in Jesus.

a. The "righteousness of God" has now been manifested for all who believe in Jesus Christ.

3:21 Here Paul returns to and begins to develop the spirited optimism of his opening announcement of the gospel as the theme of the Letter (see 1:16–17). As we have seen, it is in this gospel of God's power that the "righteousness," "justice," or "rectifying faithfulness" of God is now revealed and available to all who believe.

Paul further enlightens his audience about this marvelously new "righteousness of God." It has been fortuitously manifested "apart from the Law," that is, independently and outside of the previous principle whereby one was declared "righteous" or "just" before God by faithfully performing the works of the Law. This is fortuitous in light of the fact that no human being will be declared "righteous" before God for having accomplished the works of the Law (3:20). And yet this new "righteousness of God" is that which is "attested" or borne witness to by the scriptural "Law (Torah) and the Prophets." In other words, it represents that righteousness which the "Law and Prophets," as the written will and word of God, intended, foresaw and promised.

3:22–23 Rather than a righteousness based on doing the works of the Law, this "righteousness of God" is received and appropriated through faith in Jesus Christ and it extends to all who so believe. For, as Paul has just illustrated (1:18—3:20), with regard to being righteous before God there is no differentiation among the peoples of the world—*all* have, as a matter of fact, sinned and so *all* fall short of advancing and obtaining the esteemed "glory of God."

b. All who are justified by faith in Jesus Christ have liberation from, atonement for and forgiveness of sins.

3:24 But now, quite wondrously, *all* are freely and graciously "justified," "made righteous," by God's grace through the "redemption," the liberation from slavery to the overwhelming power of sinfulness, won by Christ Jesus. The universal power of sinfulness is thus offset by God's universal "justification" of all who believe. And so Paul is heartening his audience by bringing them back from the depths of discouragement because of the power of sin.

3:25–26 This new "righteousness of God" is by no means secretive or private. God has openly and publicly "put forth" Christ Jesus to the world as an "expiation," a means of propitiation or atonement for sins, which is acquired through faith. Christ has become such an expiation for sins not by pouring out the blood of an animal sacrifice but by pouring out his very own blood in death. By this public and open manifestation God quite effectively demonstrates his "righteousness," his "rectifying faithfulness," in forgiving sins from the past down to the present through his long-enduring forbearance. All of this distinctly and definitively demonstrates and proves beyond any doubt that God is truly and faithfully "just" and that he generously "justifies" any person who believes in Jesus.

With this more expansive explanation of his gospel in 3:21–26 Paul is convincingly coaxing his implied audience, who already share the Christian faith with him (1:8, 12), to realize the full significance and consequences of their faith. That they are now freely justified by their faith in Jesus Christ means they now have liberation from, atonement for and forgiveness of the devastating and desolating sinfulness which has engulfed them and all of humanity in absolute hopelessness. Paul is thus continuing to strengthen and encourage his audience through their mutual faith (see 1:11–12).

Along with a return to his diatribal manner of rhetorical inquiry, Paul reverts to the question of special Jewish status before God:

2. Romans 3:27–31:

27 What then becomes of boasting? It is excluded! Through what 'Law'? (The Law) of works? No, but through the 'Law' of faith! 28 For we maintain that a person is justified *by faith* without works of Law. 29 Or is God the God of Jews only? Is he not the God of Gentiles also? Yes, also of Gentiles, 30 since God is indeed One, who will justify 'circumcision' (Jews) by faith and 'uncircumcision' (Gentiles) through the same faith. 31 Do we then nullify the Law through this faith? By no means! On the contrary, we uphold the Law!

a. Justification by faith replaces justification by doing works of the Law.

3:27 The distinctive Jewish "boasting" (2:17, 23) in God based upon demonstrating one's own "faithfulness" or "righteousness" through performing the works God's Law requires is now excluded; neither Jews nor anyone else has grounds for boasting in one's own righteousness, since the new "righteousness of God" has eliminated such boasting.

Paul employs a clever play on words to forcefully assert that now a whole new principle or system involving "righteousness" is operative. Whereas he previously used the word "Law" (*nomos*) to refer to God's Law or Torah primarily as the instructions and commandments for doing the will of God, he now implements the word "Law," in a more general yet perhaps purposely ambivalent sense, to signify primarily "principle," "system" or "dispensation."[1]

And so it is not the "Law" or "principle" of the requirement to perform the works of God's Torah that has excluded "boasting" in God based on one's righteousness. No, it is the radically new "Law" or "principle" of faith that has abolished any boasting based upon the righteousness that one might establish for oneself through accomplishing the works of the Law.

3:28 For, as Paul boldly insists with emphasis on the words "by faith," a person is now "justified" or "made righteous" solely *by faith* and not by the performance of the works of the Law.

Paul further astounds and shocks his audience by undermining profoundly ingrained ideas about the relationship of "righteousness" or "faithfulness" that is to prevail between God and humanity. God has now replaced a "justification" or "righteousness" based on doing the works of the Law with his own new righteousness or justification based on faith, with novel implications and consequences yet to be seen.

To better understand Paul's next inquisitive provocations, we need to keep in mind his previous argumentation, in which he lowered all the peoples of the world to the same level of sinfulness and pinned them all in the same predicament of universal despair (1:18–3:20, 23). This is the desperate situation of all humanity before the eyes of God. And so Paul invites his readers to view and probe this dilemma from God's vantage point.

b. The One God justifies all through one and the same faith.

3:29–30 Is God the God only of the Jews, so that he should intervene only on their behalf? Of course not; God also created the Gentiles and they find themselves sinking in the same quicksand of hopelessness as the Jews. Moreover, the Jews themselves, who daily confess to the absolute oneness of God in their Shema prayer (Deut 6:4–9), would surely have to admit that there is one and the same God for Jews and Gentiles. Why should he not act the same toward both and rescue all of his created people in the same way, since all are mired in the same miserable mud? And so Paul persistently professes that this uniquely One God will justify both circumcised Jews and uncircumcised Gentiles through one and the same faith in one and the same God.

Having earlier levelled and thus unified all the peoples of the world, Jews as well as Gentiles, by wrapping them all in the same mantle of "unrighteous" sinfulness before God, Paul now correspondingly levels and thus unifies all of humanity, including especially the Jews and Gentiles who constitute his audience, by confidently proclaiming the hope that the One God *will justify* and thus "make righteous" all sinners, Jews and Gentiles, through the same faith. With this inspiring motivation Paul is beginning to challenge his readers to realize their common unity with one another and with all who believe.

c. Justification by faith actually confirms the Law of God.

3:31 But does this new principle of justification by faith mean that the Law has been tossed out the window? No, not at all. While it is true that justification by faith now supersedes justification by doing the works of the Law, the Law still has an important role to play. Although the Law has lost its power to justify, it still remains God's To-rah, it still contains instructions and commandments for doing God's will.

Paul's audience must not think that he has abrogated or invali-dated the Law with his gospel of justification by faith. On the contrary, since the Law has always represented the right way of behaving and living in relation to God and fellow human beings and has always called for faithfulness in so living, this new "rectifying faithfulness" of God, by effecting the "righteousness" the Law was intended to accom-plish, actually upholds and confirms what the Law stands for.

With his affirming assurance that we still uphold the Law and his hint that the Law has a prominent part to play in Christian life, Paul at this point has alerted his audience to expect a more precise deline-ation of the role of the Law for those justified by faith.

B. Rom 4:1–12: Abraham is the Father of All Who Are Justified by Faith.

Descent from father Abraham (see Gen 12–25) was the pride of every Jew. We have evidence elsewhere in the New Testament of a strong Jewish hope of avoiding God's eschatological "wrath" based simply upon physical descent from Abraham (see Matt 3:7–9; Luke 3:7–8; John 8:32–59). According to some Jewish traditions Abraham observed the entire Law even before it was written so that he was in-deed considered "righteous" and "justified" before God.[2] It is not sur-prising then that Paul calls his readers' attention to the eminent and exemplary figure of father Abraham. With diatribal scrutinizing Paul speaks as a Jew and from a collective Jewish perspective on Abraham:

1. Romans 4:1–8:

1 What then shall we say that Abraham our forefather according to the flesh obtained? 2 For if Abraham was justified by works, he has something to boast about, but not before God! 3 For what does the scripture say? "Abraham *believed* God and it was reckoned to him as righteousness" (Gen 15:6). 4 Now to one who works the wage is not reckoned by way of gift but by way of debt. 5 And to one who does not work but believes in him who justifies the ungodly, his faith is reck-oned as righteousness. 6 So also David pronounces the blessing on the person to whom God reckons righteousness apart from works:

7 "Blessed are those whose transgressions have been forgiven
    and whose sins have been covered;
8 Blessed is the person against whom the Lord will never
    reckon sin" (Ps 32:1–2).

a. Abraham exemplifies justification by faith.

4:1–2 What was it that made Abraham, the physical "forefather"
of every Jew, so prominent and favored in salvation history? What was
it that Abraham "found" or "obtained" through his special relationship to God? Paul convincingly persuades his audience that it was not
justification by achieving the works of God's Law. For the sake of the
argument Paul grants that if Abraham had been justified by doing
works, then he would surely have had something of which to boast.
But, as Paul jolts his audience, this was, in fact, not the case with Abraham's relation before God!

4:3 And Paul bolsters this brazen claim with the conclusive proof
of scripture. According to Genesis 15:6 Abraham *believed* God, and it
was this faith in God, not the doing of works, that justified Abraham,
since God reckoned this faith as "righteousness."

b. Justification by faith includes the blessedness of forgiveness of sins.

4:4–5 Paul utilizes the concept of working for wages to prove that
Abraham received "righteousness" not because he did works of the
Law but because he believed in God. Abraham believed in the God
who justifies "the ungodly"—those who do not properly revere God
and have no relation or any claim whatsoever on God. It was his attitude of faith that was "counted" or "reckoned" by God as righteousness, freely as a gift rather than earned as a deserved wage.

4:6–8 Paul then draws another authoritative scriptural quotation
into his argument. He joins the prophetically pronounced salvific
blessing uttered by David, esteemed psalmist and king of Israel, in
Psalm 32:1–2 to the previous quote from Genesis 15:6 by means of the
word "reckon," which they have in common:[3]

Gen 15:6: Abraham believed God and it was *reckoned* to him as righ-
           teousness.
Ps 32:2:   Blessed is the person against whom the Lord will never
           reckon sin.

This blessing, an effective proclamation of promised salvation,
Paul applies not only to Abraham but to all persons to whom God gra-

ciously reckons righteousness by forgiving their sins rather than by their performance of the works of the Law. Such persons experience the joy and hope of present "blessedness" by God not only because God has forgiven their past transgressions but also because in the future God "will *never, in no wise,*" reckon or count their sin against them. With this emphatic expression about the assured future effect of present forgiveness, Paul continues to spiritually strengthen and encourage the hope of his audience (see 1:11–12).

A crucial point in Paul's argumentation is at what time in Abraham's life was this blessing bestowed upon him? Was it before or after his circumcision?:

2. *Romans 4:9–12:*

9 Is this blessing pronounced only upon the circumcised or also upon the uncircumcised? For we say that faith was reckoned to Abraham as righteousness. 10 How then was it reckoned? While he was circumcised or while he was uncircumcised? It was not while he was circumcised but while uncircumcised! 11 For he received the sign of circumcision as a seal of the righteousness which he had by faith while he was still uncircumcised. This makes him father of all who believe without being circumcised and who thus have righteousness reckoned to them, 12 as well as father of the circumcised—those who are not merely circumcised but also follow in the footsteps of the faith which our father Abraham had while uncircumcised.

a. *Justification by faith makes Abraham the spiritual father of both Gentiles and Jews.*

4:9–10 Is God's blessing of forgiveness of sins, as promised by the psalmist David and applied to the justified Abraham, meant only for the circumcised children of father Abraham? Are we dealing with an exclusively Jewish blessing? Paul disallows any such limitation. Since Abraham's faith was reckoned to him as righteousness in Genesis 15:6, but his circumcision is not mentioned until Genesis 17:11, Paul can firmly undergird his brash assertion that Abraham was justified while he was still in a state of uncircumcision.[4]

4:11 Furthermore, Paul interprets Abraham's circumcision as merely an indicative "sign" and confirmative "seal" of the righteousness he had acquired while still uncircumcised. In other words, Abraham's sign of circumcision, while an important seal, is clearly subordinate to his justification by faith.

With such shrewd reasoning Paul daringly and brilliantly broadens and reinterprets the fatherhood of Abraham. No longer is Abraham merely the physical "forefather" of circumcised Jews (4:1). He is the spiritual father of all who are now justified and made righteous by following and imitating the faith of Abraham without being circumcised.

4:12 Abraham remains the father of the circumcised, but he becomes their spiritual father as well, provided they believe. For Abraham is their father not merely because of the physical sign of circumcision but because they imitate and share the faith he had while still uncircumcised. Paul's climax and bottom line is that now Abraham is "*our* father Abraham"—the father, the first and foremost exemplary model, of all who now believe and are justified whether circumcised or uncircumcised:

THE FATHERHOOD OF ABRAHAM

4:1:   our (Jews') forefather according to the flesh
4:11:   the father of all who believe while uncircumcised
4:12a: the father of the circumcised who believe
4:12b: our father Abraham

b. The spiritual fatherhood of Abraham unifies Jewish and Gentile Christians.

In declaring Abraham to be the father of all who are justified by believing, Paul continues his earlier thrust toward unifying his audience. In correspondence to the fact that God is not the God of the circumcised Jews only but also of the uncircumcised Gentiles (3:29–30), Abraham is not the father of the circumcised Jews only but also of the uncircumcised Gentiles. Since God now justifies all simply on the basis of faith, Jews and Gentiles are placed on equal footing before God. They share in the same saving action of God and in the same spiritual fatherhood of Abraham.

Paul is thus enlarging the mentality of his audience. Abraham is now "*our* father Abraham," the spiritual father of all of Paul's audience who believe, whether Jew or Gentile. This expanded fatherhood of Abraham prompts both the Jews and Gentiles of Paul's mixed audience to realize and be joyfully encouraged by the common unity they have as those whom God justifies because they believe.

C. Rom 4:13–25: Abraham Is the Model of Hopeful Faith for All Christians.

Continuing with his scriptural argumentation centered on Abraham, Paul elaborates upon the consequences of the new situation established since God now justifies on the basis of faith. God's powerful promise of future, final salvation is now operative and effective for those who believe:

1. Romans 4:13–16:

13 The promise to Abraham and his descendants, that they should inherit the world, arrives not by way of Law but by way of righteousness of faith. 14 If those who are adherents of the Law are to be the heirs, faith is emptied and the promise is nullified. 15 For the Law causes wrath, but where there is no Law there is no transgression. 16 This is why it is through faith, that it may be by grace, in order that the promise may be valid for all his descendants, not only for the adherents of the Law but also for those who share the faith of Abraham, who is the father of us all.

a. The promise comes to Abraham and his descendants through the righteousness of faith.

Although there are various "promises" by God to Abraham in the Hebrew scriptures—e.g., that Sarah would give birth to Isaac (Gen 15:4; 17:16, 19); the possession of the land of Canaan (Gen 12:1, 4; 13:14, 15, 17; 15:7, 18–21; 17:8); countless descendants (Gen 12:2; 13:16; 15:1–3; 17:5–6; 18:18; 22:17); blessing for all peoples of the earth (Gen 12:2–3; 18:18)—Paul is not as interested here in the *content* of the individual promises as he is in the mere *fact* of the promise as the efficacious word of God for future salvation. In fact, for Paul, as for several other authors from the same apocalyptic-eschatological milieu, "the promise" to Abraham and his descendants refers in a general way to God's promise of future end-time salvation, sometimes expressed in terms of the future and final "world" of God's making.[5]

4:13–15 Arguing again from the point of view of God's plan of salvation, Paul maintains that the promise to Abraham and his descendants of inheriting the future "world" established by God is efficacious not through the Law but through the righteousness of faith. The promise cannot be actively and validly operative through the system of adhering to the Law. Where there is Law, there is transgression of the commandments of the Law which instigates not the fulfillment of the promise but the dreadful "wrath" of God (see 2:5–8). Therefore, the promise of God cannot attain its proper function and realization through the dispensation established by the Law.

b. The promise comes through faith so that it may be efficacious for all the descendants of Abraham.

4:16 Furthermore, if adherents to the Law were to be the heirs to God's future, final "world," then the attitude of faith would be robbed of its meaning and the promise itself would be rendered impotent and ineffective. Thus, the promise must come into play within the system determined by faith, so that it can be based on the grace of God's justifying forgiveness rather than on the demand of doing the Law. In that way the promise effects its power and validity for all the descendants of Abraham, not just adherents to the Law but all who are descendants by believing like Abraham, the spiritual father of us all.

By establishing the firm validity of God's potent promise of future salvation for all who believe, Paul further informs his audience of the benefits ensuing from the faith they share with him as well as with Abraham. In addition, Paul continues to open the minds and hearts of his readers to the magnanimity of God by accentuating the unlimitedness of God's plan of salvation: The promise persists for *all* the descendants of the faith of Abraham, who is the father of *all* of "us"— Paul and his audience.

In elaborating upon the scriptural presentation of Abraham's trust in God's reliable promise, Paul highlights the tremendously strong and hope-filled faith of Abraham:

2. Romans 4:17–22:

17 As it is written, "I have established you as the father of many nations" (Gen 17:5)—in reply to this (Abraham) believed in the God who gives life to the dead and calls the things that do not exist into existence. 18 Against hope in hope he believed that he would become the father of many nations as it was said to him, "Thus will your descendants be" (Gen 15:5b). 19 He did not weaken in faith when he considered his own deadened body, about a hundred years old, and the deadness of Sarah's womb. 20 On account of the promise of God he did not doubt in disbelief but was strengthened in faith, as he gave glory to God, 21 fully convinced that what he (God) had promised he (God) was able also to accomplish. 22 This is why "it was reckoned to him as righteousness" (Gen 15:6b).

a. Abraham believed "against hope in hope" of the creative, life-giving power of God.

4:17 Paul focuses his probing spotlight on the prominent figure of Abraham ever more sharply to brightly illumine for his readers just how enormously robust total trust in God's authoritative promise can be. In humble and obedient response to God's grandly ambitious promise to make Abraham the father of "many," that is "all,"[6] nations, Abraham placed his complete trust in the awesomely magnificent creative power of God. He believed in the God who can make what is dead come to life and who can even bring into existence what has never before existed.

4:18 With a rhetorical device known as oxymoron, "against hope in hope," which is a combination of contradictory concepts into a unity, whose enhanced contradiction preserves a vigorous dramatic tension, Paul portrays the amazingly vibrant hope that accompanied Abraham's faith. It was "against hope in hope" that Abraham believed in God's bold promise to constitute him the father of all nations by granting him myriads of descendants, according to his promise that "thus," that is, countless as the stars of the heavens (see Gen 15:5), will be your descendants.

4:19 Abraham's faith was "against hope" because his own hundred year old, decrepit body was nearly lifeless and as good as "dead," surely incapable of fathering children. Moreover, his wife Sarah's womb was agedly "deadened" to barrenness, hardly offering any hope of conception.

b. Abraham's hope gained strength because of his faith in God's powerful promise.

4:20 Nevertheless, quite astoundingly and admirably, Abraham undauntedly persisted to cling to God's incredible promise and believed "in hope" based unreservedly on this promise. The emphasis within the oxymoron clearly falls on the "in hope" part of the contradiction.

Indeed, through wholehearted submission, "in hope," to the authoritative "promise of God," Abraham not only did not hesitate or waver in what would be a quite understandable disbelief, but, on the contrary, he actually experienced an increased spiritual strength in and through his act of so believing. Despite his tempting inclination to despair Abraham courageously demonstrated an entirely realistic hope, as he took into full consideration the contradiction which his weak, human situation presented for the future fulfillment of God's promise.

In addition, although Abraham saw no real possibility or hope of his ever bringing descendants into the world, he nevertheless "gave glory to God." "To give glory to God" is a fixed biblical expression, which refers not to giving God something he does not already possess, but to an active acknowledgment of God's divine mode of being, his splendor or power. And so Abraham readily acknowledged God's "glory" or authoritative "power" by permitting that power to be activated for him through his trust in God's stalwart promise. Abraham thus allowed God to be God, he allowed the divine power to work its effect within him, and so God was thereby "given glory" or "glorified."

c. Abraham's hope grew to a full conviction in the power of God.

4:21 On the emphatic note that Abraham was fully and utterly taken up and "convinced" that God was quite capable of completing what he had promised, Paul climactically sums up and concludes his colorfully vivid and enthusiastic depiction of Abraham's immensely hope-filled faith. This full conviction of Abraham expresses the complete confidence and absolute certainty that are part of his realistic and authentic attitude of hope in God's ability to fulfill his promise. And so Paul has splendidly illustrated the efficacious power of God's promise—it instigated and ignited the intensely fervent fire of hope that accompanied father Abraham's total trust in God.

d. Abraham's faith was thoroughly hope-filled.

4:22 With his dramatic display of Abraham's hardy attitude of hope Paul is insistently declaring to his audience that *this* is the kind of faith—a "fully convinced," "strengthened," "unwavering," "against hope but in hope," faith—which God reckoned to Abraham as righteousness.

With this forceful underscoring of the rugged hope that accompanied Abraham's faith Paul is well on his way toward fulfilling his previously stated purpose of spiritually strengthening and encouraging his audience (1:11–12). He is earnestly urging his audience of fellow believers, who likewise share the faith of Abraham, to be encouraged and strengthened by joining in Abraham's confident attitude of hope.

Particularly noteworthy and interesting is the way that Paul dramatically prolongs and expands upon the rather sparse biblical portrayal of the attitude of Abraham's justifying faith in Genesis 15:5–6.

Paul inserts his own extended elaboration directly between the verses of the biblical description. This clearly indicates how much Paul is concerned with elucidating the hale hope that was part of Abraham's faith. It is this highlighted hope of Abraham that is important to Paul and that he wants his readers to experience and imitate:

THE HOPE-FILLED FAITH OF ABRAHAM

4:18a: **Against hope in hope** he *believed* that . . .

4:18b: "Thus will be your descendants"   (Gen 15:5b)
          ("Abraham *believed* in God") . . .   (Gen 15:6a)

4:19a: he **did not weaken** in *faith*

4:20b: he **did not doubt** in dis*belief*

4:20c: he **was strengthened** in *faith*

4:20d: as he **gave glory** to God

4:21a: **fully convinced** (of God's powerful promise)

4:22:   "and it was reckoned to him as righteousness" (Gen 15:6b)

e. Christians embody the fulfillment of God's promise to Abraham.

Intriguing is the somewhat subtle yet quite natural and logical implication that all those who now believe, and, of course, including especially the members of Paul's audience, actually represent and embody the fulfillment of God's promise to Abraham. God promised to make Abraham the father of many = all nations (Gen 17:5 in Rom 4:17). Since Paul's implied readers are those who believe (1:8, 12) and so share in the faith of Abraham, they number among the "many" spiritual descendants of "father" Abraham (see 4:11–12, 16) and are thus constituted as genuine "heirs" together with Abraham to the promise of God's "world" to come (4:13–14). As such they are living proof that God has fulfilled and is still fulfilling his lofty promise to Abraham. This adds a cleverly captivating and compelling touch to Paul's valiant attempt to motivate his readers toward realizing and sharing the encouraging hope of their father Abraham.

Paul then turns directly to his readers and explicitly applies his stirring rendition of Abraham's hope-filled, justifying faith to their Christian faith:

3. Romans 4:23–25:

23 The words, "it was reckoned to him," were written not for him only 24 but also for us, those to whom it will be reckoned, who believe

in him who raised Jesus our Lord from the dead, 25 who was handed over to death for our trespasses but raised for our justification.

a. Christians follow Abraham's hope-filled faith.

4:23–24 Being "reckoned righteous" by faith is the point of contact between Abraham and Christians. Abraham was justified by faith; his vigorous and vibrant, hope-filled faith was reckoned to him by God as righteousness. Likewise, Christians not only have already been justified by faith (1:16–17; 3:21–26), but they can also expect in assured and confident hope that they "will" continue to "be reckoned" as righteous by God in the future.

b. The hope-filled faith of both Christians and Abraham centers on the life-giving power of God.

4:24–25 The hope-filled faith of both father Abraham and his Christian descendants centers upon the same creative, life-giving power of God. Abraham believed in the God who creates things that do not yet exist, namely his promised descendants, and who makes alive what is dead, namely his deadened body and the deadness of his wife's womb (4:17–19); the Christian believes in the God who creates new life by raising from the dead, namely by raising from the dead Jesus our Lord, whom, after he allowed him to be delivered to death for the forgiveness of our sins, he raised for our justification.

THE FAITH OF ABRAHAM AND CHRISTIANS

4:17b: (Abraham) *believed* in the God who *gives life to the dead* and calls the things that do not exist into existence.

4:24b: (Christians) *believe* in him who *raised from the dead* Jesus our Lord.

D. Summary

By employing and emphasizing the continuity between the faith of Abraham and that of Christians, Paul has convinced his audience that God justifies by faith, not by doing works of the Law (4:1–12); he has informed them of the blessedness of God's forgiveness of sins that accompanies their justification by faith (4:6–8, 25a); he has embraced his implied audience and all Christians within the universally broadened salvific domain of God (3:27–30) and the spiritual fatherhood of Abraham and thus constituted them as authentic descendants and so inheritors to the promise for God's future "world" (4:9–16); and he has ardently stimulated them toward the spiritual strength and encouragement of hope that is to accompany and result from their justifying faith.

Abraham believed in God, was justified and had hope; likewise, Paul's audience and all Christians believe in God, are justified and are likewise to have hope. Abraham exuded a realistically robust and tremendously stouthearted hope. But how is this hope to be realized and manifested in the lives of Christians, who have been justified because of the death and resurrection of Jesus Christ?

NOTES

1. J. Lambrecht, "Why Is Boasting Excluded? A Note on Rom 3,27 and 4,2," *ETL* 61 (1985) 365.

2. Sir 44:20; *Jub.* 23:10a; C. T. Rhyne, *Faith Establishes the Law* (SBLDS 55; Chico: Scholars Press, 1981) 78, 157–158 n. 80; J. Jeremias, *"Abraam,"* *TDNT* 1 (1964) 8–9.

3. Paul combines these two scriptural texts by employing the well-known Jewish exegetical method, *gezerah shawah*, the second exegetical rule of Rabbi Hillel. It consists of the mutual interpretation of two scriptural passages, which can be associated to one another through a term they have in common.

4. According to ancient Jewish rabbinic tradition Abraham was circumcised (Gen 17:10–11) twenty-nine years after the establishment of the covenant in Gen 15:10. See Str-B, 3. 203.

5. "World" expresses future eschatological salvation in the Jewish apocalyptic writing known as the *Second Apocalypse of Baruch:* ". . . and trusting with joy they hope to receive the world which you have promised them" (14:13); ". . . that they may be able to acquire and receive the world which does not die, which is then promised to them" (51:3); see also 57:1–3. And see Sir 44:21 for the idea of the promise to Abraham in terms of the "inheritance" of the world.

6. "Many" here represents the Semitic inclusive or universal "many" which is equivalent to "all"; see J. Jeremias, *"polloi,"* TDNT 6 (1968) 536–545.

Chapter V

Romans 5:1–8:39

A. Rom 5:1–11: We Christians Possess Present Peace, Grace and Hope for Future Glory.

After presenting Abraham as the prototype and paragon of God's justification by faith and concluding on the note of God's justification of Christians, Paul excites his audience with an effusive outburst announcing the beneficial consequences of that justification:

1. Romans 5:1–2:

1 Justified then from faith we have peace with God through our Lord Jesus Christ, 2 through whom we have also gained access by faith to this grace in which we now stand and we boast of our hope for the glory of God.

a. Our justification by faith brings us peace with God.

5:1 Paul draws his audience to himself and all other Christians as he heralds the "peace" that "we," all who have been justified by faith, now have with God through our Lord Jesus Christ. Based upon Paul's earlier discussions, this "peace with God" would refer, in general, to the harmony and overall well-being (the Jewish concept of "shalom"), and, more particularly, to the joyful blessedness of forgiveness that the justified Christian now experiences (3:23–26; 4:5–8, 25).

This situation of "peace with God," however, does not refer to a subjective or psychological state acquired by the believer, a feeling of "peace of mind," but rather to an objective relationship that God has freely given and established between himself and those he has justified by faith. This "peace with God" then represents the opposite of former ungodliness, unrighteousness and sinfulness which had placed all in a situation of being "enemies" subjected to the "wrath" of and thus without peace before God.

55

This serene and consoling peace comes "through our Lord Jesus Christ," through his death and resurrection for our justification (4:24–25).

b. Through faith we stand in grace and boast of our hope for the glory of God.

5:2 And it is through this Lord that all Christians have gained access to and now stand within the new situation and realm of "grace," that is, God's free and gracious bestowal of righteousness, forgiveness and reconciliation upon all who believe.

In addition, as Paul exclaims, "we" Christians "boast" of our hope for the future glory of God. And so Paul proclaims a Christian "boasting," a delightfully deep and boldly confident attitude of reliance, which replaces and supersedes former Jewish "boastings" (2:17, 23; 3:27; 4:2). Earlier Paul had unmasked Jewish "boasting" in God and the Law as a vain presumption because of their failure to live in accord with the Law (2:17–24) and thus be justified by doing the works of the Law. But now Christians, who are graciously justified by faith, possess a genuine, authentic "boasting."

We Christians boast, first of all, of our new attitude of hope for God's future salvation. The marvelous manifestation of God's salvific activity in the death and resurrection of Jesus for the justification, peace and grace of those who believe has stimulated Christians to go so far as to "boast" of their sure and certain hope of participating and sharing in the future completion of this salvific activity, in the future "glory" of God, the summation of all salvific benefits.

Not only do we Christians "boast" of our hope for the *future*, we go so far as to "boast," quite surprisingly and paradoxically, in our *present* afflictions:

2. Romans 5:3–4:

3 Not only that, but we also boast of sufferings, knowing that suffering produces steadfastness, 4 steadfastness (produces) provedness, and provedness (produces) hope.

a. We boast of our sufferings because they produce steadfastness.

5:3 "Suffering" includes not only the painful tribulations and oppression that Christians may undergo externally or internally for the sake of their faith, but also the general afflictions, distress and anguish one normally encounters in life.

Paul has baffled his readers: How can these "sufferings" invoke the joy and delight connoted by "boasting"? Even more puzzling, how can "sufferings" build a foundation for one's life before God and be the basis for the "boasting" of our sure hope of participating in God's future glory?

This perplexing paradox is explained by the actual, lived experience of Christian hope as described through a rhetorical "gradatio," a chain-like series of expressions climbing to a dramatic climax.[1] Paul is telling his audience that when we Christians who have hope encounter sufferings we experience that suffering produces for us an attitude of "steadfastness," patient perseverance or endurance which actively withstands continual opposition or distress (see Rom 8:25; 12:12; 15:4–5).

Paul is encouraging his readers, then, by reminding them that our suffering causes not a loss or destruction of hope but a transformation from hope to patient steadfastness. In other words, our suffering effectively brings about the steadfast, enduring or persevering aspect of our attitude of Christian hope.[2]

b. Our steadfastness in sufferings leads to further hope.

5:4 Paul progresses: Our steadfastness, in turn, produces "provedness," "proven character" or "the quality of being approved." That is, it places us in a state of having been tested, of having withstood trials or tribulations. Hence, Paul asserts that we Christians who have patiently endured sufferings with steadfastness experience that we have been tested and approved before God.

Finally and climactically, this "provedness," in turn, produces "hope." Paul proclaims that we Christians who have been tested and approved by steadfast suffering experience a renewal and growth of hope. Rather than eliminating hope, suffering ultimately cultivates, nourishes and revivifies our Christian hope. This is why we Christians can brashly and brazenly "boast" even of our sufferings—they actually stimulate, renew and increase the hope of which we "boast."

The experience that Paul recounts by means of this rhetorical progression of terms should not be misunderstood as a subjective or psychological process, as if illustrating the way that suffering might psychologically be the cause of hope. Rather, Paul starts with and presupposes the attitude of hope (5:2), so that what he is portraying and invoking his audience to realize is an objective experience common to Christians within or as a result of their attitude of hope.

THE PARADOXICAL GROWTH OF CHRISTIAN HOPE

5:2:   we boast of our *hope* for the glory of God

5:3:   we boast even of our *sufferings,* knowing that

        suffering produces *steadfastness,*

        steadfastness produces *provedness,*

        provedness produces (more) *HOPE.*

Similar to the illustrious hope of Abraham (4:18–21), our attitude of Christian hope remains entirely realistic. It takes into full account and embraces any and all possible sufferings one might meet throughout life.

That the inevitable afflictions of human living instigate and incite us to hope all the more assures the profound reliability, growth and strength of our Christian hope. This vibrant and vigorous hope, then, never withers or stagnates but subsists as a dynamic phenomenon always open to a new and greater growth.

It is God himself who undergirds and bolsters this bold and lively hope of Christians:

3. Romans 5:5–8:

5 And hope does not shame us, for the love of God has been poured out into our hearts through the Holy Spirit which has been given to us. 6 For while we were still weak, at this appropriate time Christ died for the ungodly. 7 Now scarcely will someone die for one who is just—though perhaps for a good person someone might dare even to die. 8 But God demonstrates his own love for us in that while we were still sinners Christ died for us.

a. God assures that our hope will never shame us.

5:5 That our attitude of hope does not "shame" us means that it does not embarrass or humiliate us by placing us in a situation of objective "shame," ridicule or disgrace before the world and before God. On the contrary, God himself upholds and guarantees the reliability of our hope, ensuring that it never becomes an empty, vain or foolish attitude. For God has profusely and lavishly "poured out" his love into our innermost being, "our hearts,"[3] through his Holy Spirit, "given" to us Christians as we now stand within the realm of divine grace (5:2). This adds a profound interior assurance to our hope (see also 8:23–25).

b. God manifests his great love for us in the death of Christ for us while we were still sinners.

5:6 What has demonstrated and still continues to demonstrate and prove God's special love for us is that precisely when we most needed it, that is, precisely while we were still hopelessly weak, ungodly, sinners (see 3:9–20, 23), Christ died on our behalf.

5:7 Paul's striking portrayal of God's love here achieves its rhetorical impact by a dazzling contrast in which God's act of love evident in Christ's death for us far surpasses even the most heroic acts of human love. Although they would be extremely rare, there may be cases in which the love of a human being might compel him to lay down his life for another "just" and "good" human being.

5:8 But God convincingly proves *his own* unique love for us Christians by the astounding and humanly inconceivable fact that Christ died for our sake precisely when we were not "just" or "good" but still weak, ungodly "sinners." It is this extreme and abundant love of God, now effusively poured into our hearts, that continually sustains our Christian hope for the glory of God, so that it never "shames" or disappoints us in any way.

Paul continues to convince and assure his audience of the utter certainty of our Christian hope for the future, based on our present status before God because of what he has accomplished for us through the death and resurrection of Christ:

4. Romans 5:9–11:

9 Now that we have been justified by his blood, how much more then will we be saved through him from the Wrath! 10 For if, while we were enemies, we were reconciled to God through the death of his Son, how much more, now that we have been reconciled, will we be saved by his Life! 11 Not only that, but all the while we are boasting in God through our Lord Jesus Christ, through whom we have now received reconciliation!

a. Our justification through the death of Christ gives us a sure hope for future salvation.

5:9–10 In two parallel expressions of exuberant hope for the future, Paul rhetorically heightens the absolute sureness of our Christian hope by employing a traditional Jewish argumentative device known as *qal wahomer*, an *a fortiori* type of logical assertion—if A is true, then "how much more" does B follow.[4] In other words, since we Christians

have now been justified by the "blood," the expiatory death of Christ
(see 3:25), "how much more then," that is, how certainly, can we hope
that "we *will be saved*" from God's dreadfully punishing "wrath"
through Christ!

Correlatively, now that we, who as ungodly sinners (5:6–8) were
once obstinate "enemies" of God, have been "reconciled" to God
through the death of his Son, "how much more," that is, how as-
suredly, do we exclaim the secure and solid hope that "we *will be saved*"
in and through his new, resurrected "life"!

The second of these two parallel proclamations of sure hope in
5:9–10 intensifies and complements the first. Whereas the first expresses future hope in terms of the more negative idea of being saved
from God's future and final "wrath," the second goes beyond this by
exclaiming future hope in terms of the more positive idea of being
saved by the new "life" we now share with the risen Lord Jesus Christ:

THE ASSURED HOPE OF CHRISTIANS

5:9:   justified . . . how much more . . . will we be saved from the
          Wrath
5:10:   reconciled . . . how much more . . . will we be saved by his Life

b. We boast directly in God because of our reconciliation through Christ.

5:11 In his climactic conclusion Paul elevates even further these
bold proclamations of Christian hope. Not only do we Christians claim
and exhibit such a confident hope for God's future salvation, but all
the while that we possess such hope for the future we are presently
"boasting" in God himself through our Lord Jesus Christ, because it is
through him that we have now received this fabulous and fantastic
"reconciliation" with God.[5]

It is God's reconciliation of sinners, which is part of his justification by faith, that firmly undergirds and bolsters our Christian hope.
Not only do we Christians delightfully and hardily "boast" of our hope
for God's future glory (5:2) and dauntlessly "boast" even of our present distressful sufferings (5:3), but, "now" that we have graciously received reconciliation from God through the death of Jesus Christ, we
are all the while joyously and confidently "boasting" in *God himself*
(5:11), the ultimate foundation and goal of all our hope.

With this audaciously enthusiastic Christian "boasting" in God
himself, Paul has arrived at the apex of his theme of "boasting." Hav-

ing earlier exposed Jewish "boasting" in God and the Law as a false and presumptuous flaunting, because Jews transgress the Law and thereby dishonor God (2:17–23), and having eliminated such "boasting" based on doing the works of the Law now that God justifies by faith (3:27; 4:2), Paul has now effectively established a true and legitimate Christian "boasting" of hope (5:2), of sufferings (5:3) and of God himself (5:11):

THE THEME OF BOASTING IN ROMANS

Former Jewish Boasting

2:17:   If you call yourself a Jew and rely upon the Law and *boast* in God . . .

2:23:   You who *boast* in the Law, do you dishonor God through transgression of the Law?

3:27:   What then becomes of *boasting*? It is excluded! Through what 'Law'? (The Law) of works? No, but through the 'Law' of faith!

4:2:   For if Abraham was justified by works, he has something to *boast* about, but not before God!

New Christian Boasting

5:2:   We *boast* of our hope for the glory of God!

5:3:   We *boast* even of our sufferings!

5:11:   And all the while we are *boasting* in God through our Lord Jesus Christ, through whom we now have received reconciliation!

In 5:1–11 Paul has explicitly drawn out for his audience his earlier implications that since a realistic and robust hope was an essential characteristic of Abraham's justification by faith (4:18–22), such a vital hope is likewise an essential consequence of the justification of us Christians, who share the faith of Abraham "our" father (4:12, 16).

Throughout 5:1–11 Paul has vigorously and vibrantly vaunted "*our*" hope as Christians. By this continual and repeated stressing in the first person plural of "*our*" completely confident Christian hope for participating in God's future salvation, Paul earnestly invites his audience to be spiritually strengthened and encouraged by this grandly assured hope that accompanies and follows from the faith "*we*" share with him (1:11–12) and all other Christians.

B. Rom 5:12–21: Our Present Situation of Grace and Hope for Life More Than Supersedes Our Former Situation of Sinfulness Leading to Death.

One of the main themes of the apocalyptic-eschatology that forms the background of Paul's thought is that of the origin of evil and the explanation of why things have gone awry in a world originally created by God as good and well-ordered. Although the universe has fallen into the grip of ungodly evil powers, evil's reign and domination over the world was thought to be temporary. It was expected that in the end-time God would rectify what has gone wrong in creation and that his final and decisive salvific activity would in some way correspond to, deal with and appropriately counter the primeval origin of evil.

Paul traces the origin of the evil apocalyptic powers of Sin and Death to the primeval, prototypical human being, "Adam." Through this one human being these powers entered the world and extended their domination to all human beings. But this first representative human being is a "type" pointing to the last representative human being through whom God restores the good order of his creation:

1. Romans 5:12–14:

12 Therefore just as through one human being Sin entered the world and through Sin Death, so also Death spread to all human beings, inasmuch as all sinned. 13 For before the Law was given Sin was in the world, but Sin is not reckoned when there is no Law. 14 Yet Death reigned from Adam until Moses even upon those who did not sin in the same way as the transgression of Adam, who is a type of the One to come.

a. Through Adam the powers of sin and death invaded the world and spread to all human beings.

5:12 After the exhilarating display of hope in 5:1–11, Paul begins to compare and contrast the new human condition dominated by grace and hope with the former human condition dominated by sin and death. The poisonous power of sin forced its way into the world through the primal sin of the one human being, Adam, the primeval human being, who representatively embodies all human beings (see Gen 2–3). Through his primal sin the contagious power of sin spread to all human beings.

The ultimate harm effected by the power of sin is the annihilating power of death. As sin entered the world, it brought with it the power of death which contagiously spread its life-destroying dominion to all human beings, since all human beings, succumbing to the inescapable power of sin, indeed sinned.

b. *The powers of sin and death prevailed even before the Law.*

5:13 And so the power of sin did not enter the world through the Law. In fact, even before the Law was handed down to Moses by God, the pervasive force of sin flourished. It merely was not yet pointed out, labeled and "reckoned" as sin by the Law, since the Law was not yet in the world.

5:14 Nevertheless, the power of death annihilated the life of all human beings from Adam to the advent of the Law with Moses. Death destroyed the life even of those who did not sin in precisely the way that Adam did, namely by transgressing a direct command from God.

But the first human being, Adam, the instigator of the destructive forces of sin and death, as a "type" or representative figure, points to and arouses the hope for the second or last, end-time Adam, the "One who is to come" as the human originator and mediator of God's grace and hope for life.

God's powerful grace unleashed through the person of Jesus Christ more than offsets and compensates for the nullifying effects of sin and death:

2. *Romans 5:15–17:*

15 But it is not the same with the gracious gift as it is with the trespass. For if through the trespass of the one the many died, how much more have the grace of God and the gift given in the grace of the one human being Jesus Christ abounded for the many. 16 And the gift is not like the consequence following from the one who sinned. For the judgment coming after one trespass brought condemnation, but the gracious gift coming after many trespasses brought justification. 17 For if through the trespass of one human being Death reigned through that one human being, how much more will those who receive the abundance of grace and the free gift of righteousness reign in life through the one human being Jesus Christ!

a. *The abundant gift of God's grace has bestowed justification upon the many who have sinned.*

5:15 Although all "the many" human beings coming after the one human being, Adam, suffered death as a consequence of Adam's sin, the grace and gift of God that is now represented by and operative in the one human being Jesus Christ outweighs by far the effects of this one sin as it "abounds" or "overflows" to all "the many" human beings.

5:16 Indeed, the gracious gift more than overbalances the results following from the one sin of Adam. Whereas God's judgment of Adam's one sin resulted in God's condemnation of all the many human beings to the destiny of death, God's gracious gift occasioned by many sins resulted in God's justification of all those who had sinned.

Paul sharpens the contrast through the parallel correspondence of key terms in 5:16:

The *judgment* coming after *one trespass* brought *condemnation;*
the *free gift* coming after *many trespasses* brought *justification.*

b. Those who have received the abundant gift of righteousness have the hope that they will reign in life through Christ.

5:17 Furthermore, whereas the annihilating power of death gained its dominating grip and "reigned" through the sin of the one human being Adam, those who now receive the overwhelming "abundance" of the gracious and free gift of God's righteousness have a supremely sure hope that they *"will reign"* in future, final "life" through the one human being Jesus Christ.

This eminently certain hope for future "life" now established through Jesus Christ thus eradicates and abundantly supersedes the despair of "death" established through Adam. The hopeless "reign" of death has now been replaced by the prospective "reign" of life.

By this multi-faceted contrast of the new situation of God's grace with the old situation of sin and death, Paul further incites and invokes his audience to join him in the hope that is now theirs as justified Christians. They are no longer doomed to despair through the "reign" of death; as those who have now received the abundantly gracious gift of God's righteousness, they may hold to the firm hope that they, not death, "will reign" through the eschatological life won for them by Jesus Christ.

Paul further develops and intensifies this richly concentrated contrast:

3. Romans 5:18–21:

18 So then, as the trespass of one human being led to condemnation for all human beings, so also the righteous deed of one human being led to the justification which is life for all human beings. 19 For as through the disobedience of one human being the many were con-

stituted as sinners, so also through the obedience of one the many will be constituted as righteous. 20 The Law came in so that the trespass might increase; but where sin increased, grace superabounded, 21 so that, as sin reigned in death, so also grace might reign through righteousness to eternal life through Jesus Christ our Lord!

a. The obedience of Christ gives all human beings the hope for future righteousness and life.

5:18 The effects of the righteous act and obedience of the one human being, Jesus Christ, correspond to, offset and reverse the consequences of the disobedience and trespass of the one human being, Adam. As surely and as inevitably as Adam's sin condemned all to a destiny of death, so surely has Christ's righteous deed justified all for a destiny of life.

And there is a definite rhetorical emphasis on the word "life" as the consequence and extension of the "justification" which offsets the "condemnation" of all.

5:19 And just as certainly as Adam's disobedience meant that all the many were established as sinners, so Christ's obedience now means the hope that all the many *will be established* as righteous.

b. God's grace has superabounded over sinfulness for the hope of eternal life.

5:20 Rather than helping the situation by lessening the sway of sinfulness, the advent of the Law actually increased human trespasses. Nevertheless, although the power of sin escalated, God's bounteous grace more than compensated for sinfulness, indeed, it "superabounded" beyond the sweeping expanse and magnitude of sinfulness.

5:21 Just as surely as the power of sin prevailed in and through its unavoidable result of human "death," so now God's powerful grace prevails in and through the righteousness which results in the sure hope for God's "eternal life" through our risen Lord Jesus Christ.

Through this concerted comparison and contrast of key concepts Paul continues to encourage and spiritually strengthen his readers (1:11–12) by demonstrating and displaying the hope for life that is now theirs as a result of God's gracious gift of righteousness.

Notice how Paul's rhetorically pointed contrasts in 5:18–21 emphasize and highlight the triumph of God's grace, righteousness and life over human sinfulness, condemnation and death:

GOD'S TRIUMPH OF LIFE OVER DEATH

Whereas the *trespass* of one led to *condemnation* for all,
the *righteous act* of one led to *justification and life* for all.
As the *disobedience* of one made the many *sinners,*
now the *obedience* of one makes the many *righteous.*
Where *sin increased,*   *grace superabounded.*
As *sin* reigned in *death,*   *grace* reigns through *righteousness*
                                        to *eternal life* through Jesus
                                        Christ our Lord.

Also noteworthy is the gradual development at this point in the Letter of the theme of Christian hope for the "life" which is an essential consequence of God's righteousness and justification by faith. It reaches a certain climax in 5:21 with the explicitly emphatic expression "eternal life":

THE CHRISTIAN HOPE FOR LIFE

1:17:   'The one who is just from faith *will live.*'
5:10:   Having been reconciled, we will be saved by his *life.*
5:17:   Those who receive righteousness will reign in *life.*
5:18:   The righteous act led to justification which is *life.*
5:21:   Grace reigns through righteousness to *eternal life.*

Paul has intensely incited his audience to the vital hope that is theirs even in the midst of the pervasive, prevailing powers of sin and death. He has vigorously illustrated and displayed a definitively certain Christian hope for God's future eternal life, a hope that effectively eradicates, totally overpowers and abundantly exceeds the dreadful despair brought about by the wicked powers of sin and death.

Can this hope for a *future* life really predominate over the *present* hopelessness we still experience because of sin and death?

C. Rom 6:1–14: We Can Now Live in Freedom from the Dominion of Sin.

With a return to the diatribal manner and style Paul engages his audience in a provocative inquiry:

1. Romans 6:1–4:

1 What then shall we say? Are we to persist in sin so that grace might abound? 2 By no means! How can we who have died to sin still live in it? 3 Do you not know that all of us who have been baptized into Christ Jesus have been baptized into his death? 4 We were thus buried together with him through baptism into his death, so that as Christ was raised from the dead by the glory of the Father, so we too might walk in newness of life.

a. We who have died to sin cannot continue to live in it.

6:1 Paul astutely averts his readers from a potential misconception and perversion of his previous assertion that the increase of sinfulness causes the power of grace to "superabound" (5:20). It would be a ridiculous parody to suppose that we should continue to sin in order to bring about an even greater increase of grace. That would mistakenly make human sin rather than God's grace the stimulus of our hope for life.

6:2 The eternal life for which we may now hope is not exclusively for the future, so that we must remain in a present life of sin. Indeed, we who have already "died to sin" certainly cannot still "live" in it. But how is it that we have "died to sin"?

b. We were baptized into the death of Christ so that we may now live a new life.

6:3–4 Paul pointedly informs his audience that when "we" were baptized as Christians, we all sacramentally participated and shared in the actual death of Jesus Christ. We were "buried," that is, totally and definitively immersed, with him by our baptism into his death. Since we were sacramentally joined with him in his death, we may also now live a new life in correspondence to the risen life he now lives after having been raised from the dead by the "glory" or power of God the Father.

By probing into and pondering the profound meaning of the death of Christ, Paul leads his audience to realize the full impact of their sacramental participation in that death:

2. Romans 6:5–10:

5 For if we have been united with him as sharers of his death, then certainly we will also be sharers of his resurrection. 6 We know that

our old self was crucified with him, so that our sinful body might be destroyed, and we might no longer be enslaved to sin. 7 For one who has died has been freed from sin. 8 If we have died with Christ, we believe that we will also live with him. 9 We know that Christ, having been raised from the dead, will never die again; death no longer has dominion over him. 10 For the death he died, he died to sin once for all, but the life he lives, he lives to God.

a. Our death with Christ in baptism gives us the hope of likewise living with him.

6:5 Union with the death of Christ through baptism assures Christians of a solid hope for likewise being united with Christ in his resurrection.

6:6 Since by baptism our former selves were actually crucified together with Christ, our "body of sin" was destroyed in that death, meaning that we are no longer inevitably and hopelessly enslaved to the dominating power of sin.

6:7 For once someone has died—as we have with Christ in baptism—he is naturally outside the realm of sin, "acquitted" of or "freed" from the sway and sweep of sinfulness.

6:8 Now by our baptism we Christians have so died with Christ, that we are firmly convinced that we will likewise live with him.

b. The power of death has been exhausted upon Christ once and for all so that he now lives an unending life with God.

6:9 Paul then shares with his audience a penetrating insight into the profound significance of the death of Christ: Since Christ has already died and been raised from the dead, he will not, indeed cannot, ever die again. Death can no longer exert its power over him.

6:10 Christ already submitted himself to the full consequence of the devastating power of sin, namely, death. The power of sin has thus been "once for all," that is, unrepeatably, completely and definitively, exhausted upon him. Death can never again deprive him of life. For the eternal, resurrection life he now lives, he "lives to God." Christ died in submission to the deadly power of sin, but he now "lives" in submission and service to God. This has reverberating consequences for Paul's audience as well as for all Christians.

Paul turns directly to his readers and inspires them to make their future Christian hope that "we *will* live with him" (6:8) an already present and "living" reality:

3. Romans 6:11–14:

11 So you also must consider yourselves dead to sin but alive to God in Christ Jesus! 12 Do not therefore let sin continue to reign in your mortal bodies, so as to obey their desires. 13 And do not any longer yield your members to sin as instruments of unrighteousness, but yield yourselves to God as those brought from death to life, and your members to God as instruments of righteousness. 14 For sin will have no dominion over you, as you are not under Law but under grace.

a. *Christians who have died to sin must live to God with Christ.*

6:11 In correspondence to the fact that Christ "died to sin" but now "lives to God," so Christians who have died with Christ in baptism may already live this same life with Christ by now considering themselves "dead to sin" but "alive to God" in and with Christ Jesus.

b. *Christians can and must surrender themselves not to the evil force of sin but to God.*

6:12 Paul urges his audience not to allow the deadly power of sin to continue to exert its destructive influence upon their mortal bodies, by submitting to the sinful desires and inclinations that are still operative in their bodies.

6:13 Playing upon the imagery of the fierce battle between the powers of good and evil prominent in the apocalyptic world view, Paul directs his troops to no longer yield the members of their bodies to the power of sin so that they become "instruments" or "weapons" for the evil force of unrighteous wrongdoing. As those who have been brought from death to life in baptism, they may now yield themselves to the superior command of God and present the members of their bodies for service to God that they may become "weapons" for the noble force of God's righteousness.

6:14 What now compels and enables Christians to do this is the supremely confident hope that the wicked power of sin "*will have no dominion*" over them, since they are not under the sway of Law but under the regime of God's mighty grace.

Paul has excited his audience with the possibility that Christians may already live, as part of their vibrant, "living" hope, the new future life for which they hope. He goes on to insist that not only is it *possible,* but it is even *necessary* for Christians to live this new life of hope now.

D. Rom 6:15–23: We Must Now Live in Freedom from the Dominion of Sin.

In the diatribal manner Paul presents his audience with a provocative query:

1. Romans 6:15–16:

15 What then? May we sin because we are not under Law but under grace? By no means! 16 Do you not know that when you yield yourselves in slavish obedience to anyone, you are slaves of the one you obey, either of sin leading to death, or of obedience leading to righteousness?

a. The new situation of grace does not permit Christians to continue in sin.

6:15 With these alluring questions Paul prevents possible misunderstandings and further clarifies the new life of Christian hope. Does the previously exclaimed hope that "sin *will not dominate*" over us, mean, then, that we are free to sin now, that "we *may* sin," within our new realm of hope founded on not being "under Law but under grace"? In other words, although it is now possible for us Christians to escape the poisonous power of sin, are we nevertheless permitted to commit sins within or even because of this new hope? "By no means!" Paul thunderously retorts.

b. Christians must become obedient slaves to the righteousness of God.

6:16 Sin and the new life of hope are completely incompatible and diametrically opposed, for if we revert to acts of sinfulness, we inevitably return to former hopelessness. That is what Paul impresses upon his audience with vivid slavery/freedom imagery, corresponding not only to a sociological reality of Paul's time but also to the "slavery" involved in being dominated by apocalyptic powers.

As Paul informs his readers, whenever they offer themselves in "slavish obedience" to anyone, they become totally dominated and indebted "slaves" of the one they "obey." If Christians return to sinning, they remain obedient slaves to sin in which their inescapable destiny is the hopelessness of future, final "death." But in the new life of hope they have become "slaves" to the "obedience" of faith in which their inevitable destiny is the hope of future, final "righteousness" before God.

Paul reassuringly urges his audience to continue to be obedient slaves to God's righteousness:

2. Romans 6:17–19:

17 Thanks be to God, that though you were slaves of sin you have become wholeheartedly obedient to the pattern of teaching to which you were committed, 18 and having been freed from sin you have become slaves of righteousness. 19 I am speaking in human terms because of the weakness of your nature. For just as you once yielded your members as slaves to immorality and to greater and greater iniquity, so now yield your members as slaves to righteousness for sanctification.

a. Christians who were once slaves of sin have been freed.

6:17 Paul reminds his Christian audience of their current status. He is grateful to God that although they were at one time hopeless "slaves" of sin, they have now begun to be obedient from the heart to the form of Christian teaching to which they were committed.

6:18 But although they have been freed *from* sin, this does not mean that they are now "free" *to* sin, for there is a sense in which they have once again become "slaves."

b. Christians must now submit themselves as slaves to the righteousness which leads to holiness.

6:19 Indeed, in the frail human terms involving the concept of "slavery," which cannot adequately express the divine reality involved here, they have again become "slaves," but this time to God's "righteousness."

Because of their weak human nature, then, inclined toward being "enslaved," Paul's audience would do well to consider themselves "slaves" to righteousness. They can and must live out their hope now, then, as a "slavery to righteousness." For just as they once slavishly submitted themselves to immorality and to wickedness which merely led to further wickedness, so now they *must* submit themselves as "slaves" to the righteousness which leads to "holiness," their sanctification by God.

By so living Paul's audience can securely assure their hope of participating in eternal life:

3. Romans 6:20–23:

20 When you were slaves of sin, you were indeed free in regard to righteousness. 21 But what benefit did you gain from the things of which you are now ashamed? For the final result of them is death. 22 But now that you have been freed from sin and have been enslaved to God, you have the fruit which leads to your sanctification, whose final result is eternal life. 23 For the wages of sin is death, but the free gift of God is eternal life in Christ Jesus our Lord!

a. In former slavery to sin Christians were destined for death.

6:20 Paul admits that when his Christian readers were still "slaves" to the power of sin, then they could have considered themselves, in a sense, "free" with regard to righteousness.

6:21 But in that situation they were bereft of any real hope for the future. He forces them to admit that they could not have expected any "fruit" or "benefit" from the sinful things of which they are now ashamed before God, since the future result of those things is merely the hopeless finality of "death."

b. Now freed from sin Christians have hope for eternal life.

6:22 But now, freed from the power of sin while at the same time "enslaved" to God, Paul informs them of their true, authentic hope for God's future, since the "fruit" or "benefit" of their living now as "enslaved" to God is "holiness" or "sanctification" from God, whose future result is eternal life.

6:23 Therefore, Paul's Christian audience can and must not continue to sin now (6:15), since the only "wages," the inevitable end product, that sin rewards is "death." But God's "free gift" produces "eternal life" for Christians in Christ Jesus our Lord. And now that they stand under the power of God's grace (6:15), Paul is convincing them that they can and must begin to live even now this future, eternal life for which they hope.

E. Rom 7:1–6: We Are Now Freed from the Imprisonment of the Law to Serve God in the Newness of the Spirit.

Now that we Christians are "under grace" we are no longer "under the Law" (6:15), and this carries consequences which Paul draws out for his readers:

1. Romans 7:1–4:

1 Do you not know, brothers—for I am speaking to those who know the meaning of law—that the Law governs a person only during that person's life? 2 For a married woman is bound by law to her husband as long as he lives; but if her husband dies, she is released from the law concerning the husband. 3 So then, she will be known as an adulteress if she belongs to another man while her husband is still living. But if her husband dies, she is free from that law, so that she is not an adulteress if she belongs to another man. 4 Likewise, my brothers, you also have been put to death with regard to the Law through the body of Christ, so that you may belong to another, to him who has been raised from the dead, in order that we may produce fruit for God.

a. The Law rules over a person only while that person is living.

7:1 Paul relies upon his audience's general and basic familiarity with the major premises of law to illustrate another important point about the efficacy of their baptismal participation in the death of Christ.

7:2–3 He quite suitably utilizes the example of the law governing marriage unions to demonstrate that the Law rules over a person only while that person is living. The key ideas in the example, which provide the points of contact for the comparison with the new situation of Christians, are that of "death" and "belonging to another." The "death" of a married woman's husband frees her from the Law so that she may quite legitimately "belong to another" man as his wife.

b. Christians have died to the Law and may now belong to Christ.

7:4 Similarly, the "death" of Christ has freed Christians, who have already died with him by their baptism (6:3–5), from the Law so that they may now "belong to another," namely, to Christ who has been raised from the dead. Since the Law has dominion only until a person has died, Paul convinces his audience that we Christians, who have died with Christ, are no longer under the domination of the Law. We now "belong" not to the Law, but to the risen Lord.

Consequently, we now can and must "produce fruit" for God, that is, our external, practical conduct can and must show forth the fruit of our inner, sacramental union with the death and resurrection of Christ. In that way, the "fruit" that we bear contributes to our future, eternal life (see 6:22).

Paul invites his readers to escape from their former captivity to the Law and now serve God in the new life of the Spirit:

2. Romans 7:5–6:

5 For while we were in the flesh, the sinful passions that come through the Law were at work in our members to produce fruit for death. 6 But now we have been released from the Law, dead to that by which we were imprisoned, so that we serve in the newness of the Spirit rather than in the oldness of the letter (of the Law).

a. The Law activated the sinful passions within us to destine us for death.

7:5 Continuing with the imagery of "producing fruit," Paul reminds his audience of our former, pre-Christian situation. When we were still "in the flesh" of trying to obey the commandments of the Law before our baptism, the Law activated the sinful passions within us "to produce fruit for death." And so, while under the dominion of the Law, we were hopelessly destined for future, final "death," the "fruit" of our life of sin (6:21).

b. Now we have been freed from the Law to serve God in the newness of the Spirit.

7:6 But now that we have been cut loose from the strangling grip of the Law, "dead" (by baptism) to that menace in which we were desperately entangled, Paul persuades us Christians that we can and must freely live out our new hope for God's future by serving God now in the "newness of the Spirit" rather than in what has now become the "oldness of the letter" of the Law.

Having set the stage, Paul will now proceed to further express and explain our extreme despair under the oldness of the letter of the Law (7:7–25) as the backdrop for his zestful and zealous proclamation of the sturdy Christian hope that is now ours as we serve God in the newness of the Spirit (8:1–17).

F. Rom 7:7–25: The Law Became the "Law" of Sin and Death for Each of Us.

Continuing with his provocative prompting in the diatribal mode, Paul audaciously challenges his audience to reflectively question the status and role played by the God-given, Mosaic Law, especially in light of Paul's previous pessimism concerning it:

1. Romans 7:7–12:

7 What then shall we say? The Law is sin? By no means! Yet I would not have experienced sin except through Law. I would not have known coveting if the Law had not said, "You shall not covet." 8 But sin, taking opportunity through the commandment, produced in me every kind of covetousness. Apart from the Law sin is dead. 9 I was once living apart from the Law, but when the commandment came, sin came to life 10 and I died; the very commandment which was meant for life turned out to be death for me. 11 For sin, taking opportunity through the commandment, deceived me and through it killed me. 12 The Law, though, indeed is holy, and the commandment is holy and just and good.

a. The Law causes each individual to experience sinfulness.

7:7 If it was through the Law that sinful passions operated within us to destine us for death (7:5), can the Law, then, actually be considered "sin"? "By no means!" Paul insistently and resoundingly roars.

To explicate the Law's role and relationship to sin, Paul aptly utilizes the first person singular, "I," to refer not just to himself but to each and every person before being baptized. He thereby rhetorically intensifies both the typicality and the personal individuality of the common experience he is describing. This causes his readers to identify more personally with the ordeal and helps Paul to hammer home more forcefully the point of the drama.

Although the Law in itself certainly cannot be considered sin, "I," Paul, each of his readers and every human being, would not have experienced the malignant power of sin had it not been for the Law. Paul forces his audience to admit that "I" would not have known the sinfulness of "coveting" if the Law had not announced, "You shall not covet" (Exod 20:17; Deut 5:21).

7:8 But it was the poisonously penetrating power of sin that slyly and stealthily took its opportunity through the commandment of the Law and awakened in "me" all manner of coveting. For without the Law sin remains "dead," that is, dormant and without its full potency.

b. Sin worked through the good Law to bring death for everyone.

7:9–10 At one time "I" (every human being) was living without the Law, but when the commandment of the Law arrived the power

of sin "came to life" and "I" in effect "died." Thus, the very commandment which was intended by God to lead to "life" actually inflicted "me" with the dismal destiny of "death."[6]

7:11 Since the Law wanted to prevent "me" from falling into the
clutches of sin and thus incurring future "death," it originally inspired
hope for "life." But in the Law's very prohibition not to sin the power
to sin became fully activated and in this way deceived "me" by taking
over, misusing and transforming the Law from a foundation for hope
into a destructive agent for the despair of "death."

7:12 Nevertheless, Paul assures his audience that the Law in itself
remains holy, and the commandment holy, just and good.

Paul points the finger at the venomous power of sin, rather than
the Law, as the culprit in our predicament:

2. Romans 7:13–16:

13 Did that which is good, then, become death for me? By no
means! But it was sin, to show itself as sin, which produced death in
me through what is good, in order that sin might become sinful to the
extreme through the commandment. 14 For we know that the Law is
spiritual; but I am fleshly, sold in bondage to the power of
sin. 15 What it is I actually accomplish, I do not even realize. For I do
not do that which I want, but the very thing I hate, this I do. 16 If then
I do that which I do not want, I agree that the Law is good.

a. Sin magnified its sinfulness by producing death for every individual through the good Law.

7:13 Paul asks his audience if we are not compelled to admit that
what is in itself "good," namely the Torah, the Mosaic Law from God,
has actually become for "me" (each human being) the cause for the
despair that is "death"? "By no means!" is Paul's vehement and vocif-
erous rejoinder. For it was sin, in order that it might manifestly prove
itself to be sin, that destined "me" for death through the "good" Law,
so that sin might become ever more excessively sinful through the
commandment.

b. The good and spiritual Law cannot prevent the individual from becoming enslaved to the deadly power of sin.

7:14 It is the common knowledge of Paul and his audience that
the Law is "spiritual." But the Law, as a "spiritual" reality, simply lacks
the power necessary to effect within the "fleshly" individual the life it
was originally meant to stimulate and establish. Although the Law tries

to help by commanding "me" not to sin, it remains helplessly powerless to prevent "me" from being completely "sold under" and enslaved to the deadly power of sin.

7:15 So much am "I" in bondage to the power of sin that "I" do not even realize what it is that "I" manage to achieve; "I" am not even aware of the full extent of the sinfulness that "I" may be bringing about. For "I" do not do what "I" want to do, namely, God's life-bringing commandment, but what "I" hate, namely the transgression of God's will, this is what "I" in fact finally accomplish!

7:16 Thus, if "I" actually bring about the sinfulness that "I" do not really want to achieve, "I" am thereby led to agree that the Law is certainly "good," since it tries to prevent "me" from doing what "I" hate. Although "I" am able to agree with the "good" Law, shackled as "I" am by the power of sin, "I" am simply unable to perform the good that the Law commands.

Paul continues to single out and pin the blame for this wretched situation on the power of sin which dwells deep within every individual:

3. *Romans 7:17–20:*

17 So then it is no longer I who accomplish this, but sin dwelling within me. 18 For I know that good does not dwell within me, that is, in my fleshly self. Although I can readily will it, I can in no way accomplish what is good. 19 For I do not do the good that I want, but the evil that I do not want is what I practice. 20 If then I do that which I do not want, it is no longer I who accomplish this, but sin dwelling within me.

a. *The overwhelming power of sin dwells within each individual.*

7:17 As the drama builds, Paul impresses upon his audience just how thoroughly overwhelming and oppressively permeating the deceptive power of sin is. It extends to the very interior, the core, of the human person, and so overpowers the individual that it is not even "I" who accomplish the sin "I" hate but the excessive power of sin itself dwelling within "me."

b. *The indwelling power of sin forces each individual to do undesired evil.*

7:18–19 By his dramatic depiction of the universal experience of the power of sinfulness, Paul constrains his audience to realize and identify with this common weakness of the human condition. The individual human person experiences that the power to sin rather than to do good seems to subsist within him or her. The mere will to perform the good advised by the Law and ardently desired by the individual is, alas, far from adequate to offset and overcome the penetrating, indwelling power of sin as the root cause of this hopeless human quandary.

7:20 As Paul emphatically repeats, it is the indwelling power of sin that has conquered every individual and rendered him/her powerless from within.

With a vividly graphic characterization of the ferocious inner battle that rages between the conflicting forces of good and evil within the individual, Paul reaches the heart-rending, lamentful climax of his insightful and compelling portrait of the human dilemma of despair:

4. Romans 7:21–25:

21 So I find it to be a "Law," when I want to do the good, that the evil lies readily at hand for me. 22 For I delight in the Law of God with respect to my inner self, 23 but I perceive another "Law" in my members at war with the "Law" of my mind and making me captive to the "Law" of sin which is in my members. 24 What a wretched person I am! Who will rescue me from this body of death? 25 Thanks be to God through Jesus Christ our Lord! So then, it is I myself who serve the Law of God with my mind but the "Law" of sin with my flesh.

a. Each individual is imprisoned by the indwelling "Law" of sin.

7:21 With several clever and perceptive plays on the word "law" (nomos) Paul underscores for his readers the pathetic powerlessness of the Mosaic Law, the Torah, to combat the apocalyptic forces of evil which have ingrained themselves deep within the individual. This Law simply cannot rescue the individual from the dilemma of despair brought on by the "extreme sinfulness" (7:13) of the power of sin. On the contrary, another "Law" seems to come into play and take over the individual. Thus, when "I" (every person) want to do what is good and in accord with God's will and Law, "I" discover a different "Law" to be operative, namely the "rule" or "principle"[7] that evil lurks readily close by for "me."

7:22–23 Although the individual, "I," can delightfully and readily agree with the Law of God according to "my inner self"—my mind, heart and conscience—"I" experience another "Law,"[8] a driving force or power within my bodily self, which strongly conflicts and does vicious battle with the "Law" of my mind (the Law of God with which I agree).

This wickedly antagonistic "other Law" renders "me" feebly captive (see 7:6) to what has now become the "Law" of sin, the Mosaic Law as misused, dominated and transformed by the power of sin, that "I" now experience within my bodily self. The individual, then, finds himself/herself helplessly and hopelessly entangled and entrapped by the ruthless power of sin that has so poisoned the Law that it now viciously torments and tears apart one's inner self.

b. Jesus Christ has rescued each individual from serving the death-bringing "Law" of sin.

7:24 Paul has finally arrived at the critical low point of his dramatic demonstration of the dilemma of despair with regard to sin and the Law. By dragging his audience through the universal experience of the overwhelming power of sinfulness that every individual human being undergoes and can easily identify with, Paul has forced his readers to taste of the helplessness and drink deeply of the utter desolation of this predicament. He has caused them to confront the perplexing problem that the good and spiritual Law of God, which tried to induce hope for life by prohibiting sin, and with which "I" could interiorly agree, is the very same Law that the power of sin dwelling within my inner being has deceptively transformed into the "Law" of sin for "me."

Having perched his readers on this road to hopelessness, tossed them into this ocean of gloom and dropped them into the dark and abysmal pit of misery, Paul invites them to scream out with him in lamentful anguish: "What a wretched person I am! Who will rescue me from this body of death?"

7:25 Immediately Paul interjects a spontaneous, preliminary reply, already expressing the gratitude for and assuring his audience of the solution to this desperate plea for deliverance from the despair of death—"thanks be to God through Jesus Christ our Lord!"

But before plunging his readers into an invigorating proclamation of the saving Christian hope which answers their excruciating cry of hopelessness, Paul succinctly sums up this absolute dilemma of despair in which the individual "I" was totally entrapped and enslaved before being set free by Christ in baptism. In one final thrust Paul requires his readers to empathize and commiserate with the common plight of every individual, torn between the contradictory forces which push and pull him/her: On the one hand, "I" serve the Law of God with my mind, but, on the other hand, this very same "I" serves the "Law" of sin with my flesh.[9]

G. Rom 8:1–17: But the "Law" of the Spirit of Life Has Freed Each of Us from the "Law" of Sin and Death.

In answer to the previous lamentful plea for rescue from the agonizing misery of being destined for future, final death, Paul energetically refreshes and rouses his readers by reminding them of their new Christian hope:

1. Romans 8:1–4:

1 But there is no condemnation now for those in Christ Jesus! 2 For the "Law" of the Spirit of life in Christ Jesus has freed you from the "Law" of sin and death! 3 What the Law, weakened because of the flesh, was unable to do, God did—sending his own Son in the likeness of sinful flesh and as atonement for sin, he condemned sin in the flesh, 4 so that the requirements of the Law might be fulfilled by us, who behave not according to the flesh but according to the Spirit.

a. The "Law" of the Spirit of life in Christ has freed each individual from condemnation under the "Law" of sin and death.

8:1 With a reassuring surge Paul soothes the burning consternation he has embroiled his audience in by announcing that there is now no condemnation to death for all Christians who have been joined to Christ Jesus by baptism.

8:2 Now a new "Law" of the Spirit of life in Christ Jesus has wonderfully liberated "you," the individual "I" representative of every person who wails the woeful lament of 7:24, from the imprisonment of the "Law" of sin and death.

This new "Law" of the Spirit of life refers to the order, rule and directives for how we are now to live as determined and dominated by the power of God's Spirit rather than by the power of sin (see 7:14–23).[10] Living by this "Law" of God's Spirit will thus lead us to future, eternal "life" with Christ Jesus, since it has freed us from the "Law" of sin, God's directives for proper living now dominated and transformed by the power of sin and thus leading to future, final "death." We Christians, then, have been extricated from the miserable, miry morass of despair due to sin and death!

b. God condemned sin by sending his Son so that we Christians may live by the Spirit.

8:3 As Paul explains, it was God himself who graciously remedied the inability of his good and spiritual Law (7:14) to lead us to "life" (7:10), after it had been weakened through the flesh, the sinful human condition. He sent his very own Son into this human condition, in the "likeness"[11] of sinful flesh, for the purpose of removing or atoning for sin and thereby condemned sin directly in the flesh.

This is what bolsters the assurance for Paul's readers that there is truly "no condemnation" for them now: God has already "condemned" sin, the root cause of our former condemnation to death (5:16, 18; 7:23–24), precisely where the power of sin was operative—"in the flesh." God condemned sin and thus eliminated its power to bring about "death" through the death to sin of his Son (6:9–10) sent in the likeness of the very same human flesh that the power of sin had previously dominated.

8:4 Since God has eradicated sin's deceitful power over us, we Christians are now enabled to perform and fulfill the just requirements of God's Law. And so Paul prods his Christian readers to conduct their lives no longer in accord with their sinful human condition but in accord with the power of God's Spirit.

Paul further elucidates why his audience can and must now live under the power of God's Spirit:

2. Romans 8:5–8:

5 For those who live according to the flesh strive for the things of the flesh, but those who live according to the Spirit strive for the things of the Spirit. 6 The striving of the flesh results in death, but the striving of the Spirit results in life and peace. 7 For the striving of the flesh is enmity against God; it does not submit to the Law of God, for indeed it cannot. 8 Those who live in the flesh cannot please God.

a. Christians must strive for the concerns of the Spirit.

8:5 In line with his apocalyptic-eschatological milieu Paul sets up a strict dualism between those who still live according to the "flesh," the sinful human condition, and those who live according to the "Spirit" of God. Paul persuades his listeners to shun the former group and adhere to the latter. Otherwise, they will not be living in accord with their new Christian hope, but will descend into previous hopelessness.

b. Striving for the Spirit brings life, peace and the pleasing of God.

8:6 For Paul warns that those who strive or aspire for the concerns of the flesh are actually striving for a sure and inevitable "death," final and definitive separation from God. But those who strive for the concerns of the Spirit are definitely on their way to a secure "life and peace" with God.

8:7–8 Since the striving of the sinful human condition, the "flesh," is diametrically opposed to God, it is absolutely impossible for those who live in accord with their human "flesh" to obey the Law, God's directives for how to live in such a way as to please God and thus have hope for future life with God.

But Paul turns directly to his Christian auditors and makes them realize that they have been totally transformed by the dwelling of God's Spirit within them:

3. Romans 8:9–11:

9 Now you are not in the flesh but in the Spirit, inasmuch as the Spirit of God dwells within you. For anyone who does not have the Spirit of Christ does not belong to him. 10 But if Christ is in you, although your bodies are dead because of sin, your spirits are living because of righteousness. 11 If the Spirit of him who raised Jesus from the dead dwells in you, he who raised Christ from the dead will give life to your mortal bodies also through his Spirit dwelling within you.

a. Christians are spiritually alive through the indwelling of the Spirit.

8:9 Within the apocalyptic dualism of "flesh" opposed to "Spirit" Christians can now live under the realm determined by the Spirit, since the Spirit of God dwells directly and deeply within Christians who belong to Christ by their baptism.

Since they now have the Spirit of Christ, Paul's readers and all Christians, in belonging to Christ, are situated within a whole new sphere of power and influence. Since Christ now subsists within their very persons, the intense apocalyptic battle, in which each individual experiences the push and pull of the contradictory forces of good and evil within oneself, is able to be overcome.

8:10 Even though their physical bodies are virtually "dead" and will inevitably undergo death because of the corrupting power of sin (see 7:17, 20, 23–24), Paul enthusiastically spurs on his listeners by insisting that their spiritual selves are now alive and well because of the gift of "righteousness" they have received from God.

b. The indwelling of the Spirit gives Christians the hope for future life with God.

8:11 Furthermore, since the Spirit of the God who has already raised Jesus Christ from the dead now dwells deep within their individual persons, Paul energetically sparks their spirits with the solidly secure and assured hope that with this very same life-giving power this very same God *"will give life"* also to their still mortal persons through his Spirit which dwells within them. Paul insists, then, that Christians are not only spiritually alive now but will also surely attain future life with God as well.

There are definite consequences for how Christians are to conduct themselves now in view of their wonderfully new standing and status before God:

4. Romans 8:12–17:

12 So then, brothers, we are debtors not to the flesh, to live according to flesh. 13 For if you live according to flesh, you are destined to die, but if by the Spirit you put to death the deeds of the body, you will live! 14 For all those who are led by the Spirit of God are sons of God. 15 For you did not receive a spirit of slavery reverting you back into fear but you received a spirit of sonship by which we cry out, 'Abba! Father!' "16 The Spirit himself bears witness with our spirit that we are children of God, 17 and if children, then heirs, heirs of God and fellow heirs with Christ, inasmuch as we suffer with him in order that we might also be glorified with him.

a. Putting to death sinful conduct assures Christians of a hope for life.

8:12–13 Drawing his audience closely to him in fraternal affection, Paul adamantly urges and insists that their moral lives can and must now correspond to their Christian hope. He alerts and warns them not to continue to live under the perverse influence of their sinful human "flesh," otherwise they are doomed to the inescapable, annihilating finality of death. But if by God's Spirit they avoid sinfulness and "put to death" their sinful conduct, Paul guarantees them of the sure and secure hope that thereby *"you will live!"*

b. By the Spirit Christians are privileged to be sons of God and heirs with Christ of future glory.

8:14 Paul encouragingly enlightens his listeners that they whose lives are now influenced and determined by God's Spirit have graciously been favored with the new and splendid status of actually being "sons of God."

8:15 With a play on the sociological difference between "slaves" and "sons" Paul apprises his audience that by reason of their baptism they are no longer "slaves" shackled with a spirit of slavery intimidating them again with the terrible fear of eschatological death that engulfed them while they were still helplessly enslaved to the "Law" of sin and death (see 7:6, 23–24; 8:2). No, they are now "sons" endowed with a spirit of sonship, which entitles them to join Paul and all other Christians in the fearless and confident cry, "Abba![12] Father!"

8:16–17 God's Spirit assures us Christians interiorly in our own spirits that since we are now already "sons" and "children" of God, we are also "heirs of God" and "fellow-heirs with Christ" so that we may cling to the firm and fearless hope of inheriting a future status with God as well.

The chain of slavery leading to fear of the future has been broken and replaced with a chain of sonship (sons-children-heirs-heirs of God-fellow heirs with Christ) leading to hope of inheriting God's future world. The persistent distress and suffering that all Christians experience aligns them with the suffering of Christ and thereby fashions them into "fellow-heirs with Christ." This means that since we Christians suffer along with Christ we are destined to likewise be glorified together with him.

After Paul had thoroughly discouraged and disheartened his listeners by confronting them with the fearful fate that was theirs due to the absolutely overwhelming domination of sinfulness in their lives (7:7–25), he has now heartened and invigorated their lives by instilling within them a hopeful expectation for the brilliance of God's future glory (8:1–17).

H. Rom 8:18–39: We Can Be Absolutely Assured That Our Future Glory Will Far Surpass Our Present Sufferings.

Leaping forth from the hope he has just pronounced, Paul soars to its summit as he boldly and lustily illustrates and proclaims the complete and utter assurance that Christians may possess of the magnificence of God's glorious future over the misery of the present:

1. Romans 8:18–22:

18 I am convinced that the sufferings of the present time are not comparable to the coming glory to be revealed unto us! 19 The eager expectation of creation awaits the revelation of the sons of God. 20 For creation was subjected to futility, not of its own accord but because of the one who subjected it, in hope. 21 Indeed even creation itself will be freed from slavery to corruption for the glorious freedom of the children of God. 22 For we know that all creation groans together and travails together even until the present time.

a. *Our future glory will far exceed our present sufferings.*

8:18 Paul adds the authoritative weight of his own personally impassioned and strong "conviction" about God's future glory to impress upon his readers the assurance of their Christian hope. He himself is fully convinced that the future glory which God will lucidly reveal to us cannot be compared to, that is, it will more than compensate for and far surpass, the sufferings we Christians presently experience.

By means of a clever "catch-word" connection involving the words "suffer" and "glory," this earnest conviction of Paul bolsters and carries forward his previous pronouncement that since we Christians necessarily and inevitably suffer with Christ, we will surely likewise be glorified with him:

PAUL'S CONVICTION OF GLORY OVER SUFFERING

8:17:   . . . we *suffer* with him in order that we might also be *glorified* with him.
8:18:   *I am convinced that . . .*
            the *sufferings* of the present time are not comparable to the coming *glory* to be revealed unto us!

This brash conviction of Paul serves as the bold headline eloquently enunciating the thesis and theme of the remainder of this section of the Letter.

b. *Even creation itself strains and strives forward in hope of the glorious future of God.*

8:19 By steering his audience to resonate with the eager hope now evident in all of creation, Paul not only illustrates the fervent intensity and all-embracing extensiveness of our hope but also broadens the basis for him to convince his listeners of the complete certainty they may have of attaining the future glory for which they ardently hope.

So great and so sure is "the coming glory to be revealed to us" that even creation itself has an "eager expectation" which "awaits" the future "revelation of the sons of God." Creation's "eager expectation" and "awaiting" elucidate the intensely expectant, forward-looking and earnest character of a hope intently concentrated toward the future of God.[13] This hope of creation is intimately related to that of Christians; it urgently looks forward to the same future that Christians await, the "revelation of the sons of God," the future completion of the present status of Christian sonship (8:14–17).

8:20 Creation eagerly expects and awaits God's future glory because, in accord with apocalyptic-eschatological thinking, it had long been subjected to "nothingness" or "futility." That God allowed creation to be subjugated to utter futility means that it was destined to future nothingness, to a failure to achieve its original God-given purpose, the "glory" for which it was created.

This oppressive subjection was not a matter of creation's own doing or willing, but happened "because of the one who subjected it," which probably refers to Adam, the representative of humankind, whose transgression allowed the power of sin to enter the world (see 5:12–14) and extend its poisonous effects throughout the whole of creation (see Gen 3:15–19). But although creation was subjected to futility, it was subjected *"in hope."*

8:21 Indeed, creation has the eager and earnest hope that *"it will be freed"* from its slavery to corruption by participating in "the glorious freedom of the children of God."

This further indicates how closely the hope of creation is intertwined and oriented to that of Christians, who likewise ardently await the glorious future completion of their present freedom as God's children (8:16–17). Here Paul is boosting the hope of his readers; they are to be duly impressed, inspired and spurred on by the fact that Christian hope extends to and embraces *even creation itself!*

And that "even creation itself" will participate in the future, final freedom which God will establish and reveal to us illustrates the truly unexcelled greatness of God's "coming glory."

8:22 As is clearly evident to Paul's audience, all of creation, long ago subjected to futility in hope, is still "groaning together" and "travailing together" even at the present time.

This "groaning together" of all creation expresses the hope of creation in terms of a deep and intense, lamentful sighing, a longing or yearning to be liberated from present enslavement. Thus, this "groaning" of all creation is a hopeful striving forward to God's future glory.

And all of creation's groaning together is reinforced by its "being in travail together," an expression of acute suffering or agony, as in the process of giving birth. There are Old Testament and Jewish apocalyptic traditions in which "birth-pangs" refer to the sufferings or "woes" out of which the messianic age is given birth. Just as for "groaning," there is an inherent expectation and future orientation to this "travailing," as it looks forward to the end of present pain in the joy of the future "birth." The "travailing together" of all creation then is a present suffering, a straining forward, which looks in hope to the future, final glory of God.

Paul has compelled his listeners to realize that all of creation hopes. Because creation had been subjugated to utter futility, this hope emerges as an "eager expectation" which "awaits" in "groaning and travailing." This hope, then, is a kind of suffering in hope, a hopeful suffering, a painful striving and straining beyond itself for God's final freedom from futility. Paul's audience must stand in awe: How truly great the future glory of God must be, if *all* of creation from long ago even *until now* "groans and travails" in hope of it!

THE HOPE OF ALL CREATION

8:19:   The *eager expectation* of creation *awaits* the revelation of the sons of God.

8:20:   Creation was subjected to futility . . . *in hope.*

8:21:   Creation itself *will be freed* from slavery to corruption for the glorious freedom of the children of God.

8:22:   All creation *groans together* and is in *travail together* even until now.

We Christians participate in the general hope of all of creation, as we likewise groan for and await final sonship and liberty:

2. *Romans 8:23–25:*

23 Not only that, but we ourselves having the Spirit as first-fruits, we also groan within ourselves as we await sonship, the redemption of our body. 24 In hope we were saved, but a hope that is seen is not hope. 25 For who hopes for what he sees? But if we hope for what we do not see, we await it with steadfastness!

a. Along with creation Christians who have the Spirit strive forward in hope of future sonship and redemption.

8:23 Paul excitedly proclaims that this extensive, vibrant and dynamic hope now evident in all of creation embraces the hope of all Christians. Already possessing the gift of God's Spirit as the "first-fruits," that is, a first installment which guarantees a future completion, we "groan" deep within ourselves as we eagerly "await" the guaranteed completion of our "sonship" and the "redemption" of our bodies.

This "sonship" refers to the decisive and definitive fulfillment of the sonship we Spirit-gifted Christians already claim (8:14–17). It corresponds to the "revelation of the *sons* of God" for which creation awaits in hope (8:19).

In apposition to this sonship, the "redemption of our body" further expresses God's future salvation which we Christians await. It denotes God's final liberation of our mortal bodies in whom the Spirit now dwells (8:11). This "redemption" thus corresponds to the "glorious freedom of the children of God," the future goal of the hope of all of creation (8:21).

Paul further elucidates how the hope of his Christian readers is closely attuned to the hope of creation: Just as in the hope of all creation so there is a "groaning" or suffering aspect in Christian hope. Our hope as Christians who have received the Spirit takes the form of an inner, lamentful "groaning," that is, a hopeful *suffering* or a *suffering* hope, because of the inevitable sufferings of this present age (8:18), and because of the mortal condition of our bodily existence (8:11, 23), not yet fully and finally "redeemed" (8:23) or "liberated" (8:21). But this interior "groaning" is at the same time a *hopeful* suffering or a suffering *hope* because we Christians already possess God's Spirit as the "first-fruits" which guarantees the future completion of the salvation we Christians "await" even as we "groan."

b. Christians were saved in hope of a yet unseen future.

8:24 With an eloquent explication of the great goal of our Christian hope Paul exhilarates his audience into clinging to and displaying with patient steadfastness the hope that is ours. As Paul explains, it was *"in hope"* that "we were saved." In other words, we were saved so that we are now in a situation of hope; we were saved so that we can and must exhibit an attitude of hope; we were saved so that now we are open to an unseen and yet to be revealed future salvation.

In definition-like style Paul enthralls his listeners with a cogent description of the future goal of our hope: A "hope" that can be seen is simply not "hope." Indeed, no one "hopes" for something that can be seen. If the goal of hope partakes of this earthly, human, physically visible realm, then it cannot be the true goal of the hope we Christians claim. Our hope looks forward not to what is presently visible but to the future, invisible, divine realm.

Light is shed on the meaning of what is "seen" as opposed to what is "unseen," as the future goal of hope, by Paul's statement in a similar context of hope in 2 Cor 4:18: "Because we look not to the things that are seen but to the things that are unseen; for the things that are seen are transient, but the things that are unseen are eternal." These transient "things that are seen" characterize the short time of affliction expressed in 2 Cor 4:17, which is bringing about an "eternal" weight of "glory" beyond all comparison, characterized by the "eternal things that are unseen." Thus, the "things that are seen" relate to the sufferings of this present age; and the "things that are unseen" relate to the future, eternal glory of God.

The ideas and context of hope in 2 Cor 4:17–18 closely approximate Rom 8:18, 23–25, in which Paul likewise depicts the hope of Christians for the coming glory of God which will far excel present sufferings (compare Rom 8:18 with 2 Cor 4:17). As in 2 Cor 4:17–18, then, the things that we now see (Rom 8:24) embrace the sufferings of this present time (8:18) and thus are in no way the goal of our hope.[14]

c. Christians await their unseen future hope with steadfastness.

8:25 Paul prods and incites his listeners to "eagerly await with steadfastness" the future goal of the hope that we do not yet see. The true goal of Christian hope is "what we do not see," the future, eternal, invisible glory of God. As the goal of our hope, "what we do not see" further describes and explains the sonship and redemption for which we groan and await (8:23).

And just as "what we do not see" corresponds to the "coming glory to be revealed to us," so also "with steadfastness" corresponds to the "sufferings of the present time" (8:18). Paul assures that we Christians can eagerly await what we do not see "with steadfastness," with an attitude of active, persevering endurance over and against the "sufferings of the present time," because the unseen, future glory of God for which we hope will abundantly exceed any sufferings we presently encounter.

To sum up our Christian hope, because we Christians have already received the indwelling gift of God's Spirit in this time of necessary and inevitable sufferings (8:18), we "groan" within ourselves, lamentfully longing and yearning, as we "await" God's future and final liberation of our presently oppressive existence (8:23). But because of the overwhelming greatness of the "unseen," future glory of God for which we, who have already been saved, can and must now hope, as Paul unabashedly proclaims, we do indeed hope as we "eagerly await" this future of God "with steadfastness" against present sufferings (8:24–25).

THE HOPE OF CHRISTIANS

8:23:   We *groan* within ourselves as we *await* sonship, the redemption of our bodies.

8:24:   In *hope* we were saved, but *hope* that is seen is not *hope* . . .

8:25:   As we *hope* for what we do not see, we *await* it with *steadfastness!*

Paul continues to inspire and motivate his readers to an assured hope by further delineating the role played by God's Spirit dwelling within us:

3. Romans 8:26–27:

26 Likewise the Spirit also helps us in our weakness; for we do not know how to pray as we ought, but the Spirit himself intercedes on our behalf with wordless groanings. 27 And he who scrutinizes hearts knows what the striving of the Spirit is—that he intercedes for the saints according to God's will.

a. The indwelling Spirit helps hopeful Christians to pray.

8:26 Not only does the gift of God's Spirit as the "first-fruits" instigate our inner groaning in hope for God's future, but this same indwelling Spirit helpfully intercedes for us with "wordless groanings." Precisely because the goal of our hope is the invisible, future glory of God, it is humanly impossible for us to know how to pray for it. But our inner "groaning" in hope is accompanied by the interior, "wordless groanings" of the Spirit, which, as humanly inexpressible utterances, are quite appropriate intercessions for the humanly "unseen" future of God.

b. The Spirit intercedes so that the prayers of Christians accord with God's will for the future.

8:27 The all-knowing God, who probes our inner beings, our hearts, understands these wordless groanings; he knows the inner "striving" of the Spirit, for it is in correspondence to the divine will that the Spirit intercedes for us Christians, the "saints."[15] With these interior "groanings" in accord with the unseen, future completion of God's will, the Spirit assists and thereby enables us to pray for the future goal of our hope.

And so Paul pushes his readers to pray in hope for God's future and makes them even more certain of the attainment of their hope: If the Spirit intercedes with our praying as we await with steadfastness, then we are guaranteed of arriving at the unseen, future goal of our hope (8:25) and assured that its glory will far exceed our present sufferings (8:18).

Ever more boldly and brazenly, Paul securely anchors the absolute assurance of our Christian hope by inserting our attainment of hope's future goal into the certainty of God's eternal plan of salvation:

4. Romans 8:28–30:

28 We know that all things work together for the good for those who love God, those who are called according to his purpose. 29 For those whom he foreknew he also predestined to be conformed to the image of his Son, in order that he might be the first-born among many brothers. 30 Those whom he predestined he also called; and those whom he called he also justified; and those whom he justified he has also glorified!

a. God makes all things work together for the final "good" of those who love him.

8:28 Paul obliges his listeners to admit that we Christians will definitely arrive at the future goal of our hope because it is God himself who has absolutely assured it: First, as Paul and his audience realize, God makes everything in his creation work together for "the good," that is, for final salvation or glory, for the benefit of us who love God and are called in accord with his purpose (see 1:6–7). And so God guarantees our participation in the final fulfillment of his salvific purpose.

b. God has predestined Christians to share in Christ's Sonship.

8:29 Second, from the very beginning of his plan of salvation, God has predestined us "to be conformed to the image of his Son," that is, to share in the future, final glory of the risen, heavenly Christ, and so to be among all the many brothers and sisters of his first-born Son (see 8:14–17).

c. God will surely bring all Christians to final glorification.

8:30 And third, God will definitely bring to final glorification all of us Christians, whom he has already "predestined," "called" and "justified." It has already been definitively decided within God's eternal plan of salvation, a divine process which has already commenced and so will relentlessly reach its culmination.

That God, in effect, "has glorified" us already serves as the emphatic climax to the rhetorically powerful, chain-like "gradatio" (see 5:3–4) which epitomizes God's on-going activity from the beginning to the end of his total plan of salvation:

CHRISTIAN ASSURANCE OF FINAL GLORIFICATION

8:30:   Those whom he predestined, he also called;
         those whom he called, he also justified;
         those whom he justified, he has also GLORIFIED!

And so, that God "has glorified" us already firmly guarantees our participation in the coming "glory" to be revealed unto us, which will far surpass the sufferings of the present (8:18), so that we Christians may indeed "eagerly await it with steadfastness" (8:25). Paul is thus propelling his audience to possess an indubitable certainty about their Christian hope.

As Paul continues to convince and motivate his listeners toward the absolutely assured hope that all Christians can confidently claim, he returns to the diatribal style with a bluntly rhetorical interrogation:

5. Romans 8:31–34:

31 What then shall we say in view of these things? If God is for us, who is against us? 32 He who did not spare his own Son but gave him up for us all, will he not give us all things together with him? 33 Who will bring a charge against God's elected ones? It is God who justifies! 34 Who is to condemn? It is Christ Jesus who died, but indeed was raised, who is at the right hand of God, and who intercedes for us!

a. We Christians have the sure hope that God who already gave us his Son will also give us complete and total salvation.

8:31 Here Paul bursts forth with an electrifying salvo of questions and exclamations which caps off and culminates all that he has been proclaiming throughout Romans 5—8. As he has been dazzlingly demonstrating to this point, God is most definitely, totally and wholeheartedly, on our side. Since God has revealed how much he is "for us," in any situation of judgment, trial or judicial process there is simply no one who can possibly prevail "against us."

8:32 Indeed, it was God who gave us his very own Son in death "for us" all. With this undeniable evidence of how much God has already done "for us" in giving us his own Son, Paul convincingly asserts the firm hope that therefore he surely *will give* us, together with Christ, "all things," that is, the totality and completion of God's future, definitive salvation.

The encompassing designation, "all things," succinctly and climactically recapitulates all of Paul's previous expressions of the future goal of our hope throughout 8:18–32:

THE FUTURE GOAL OF CHRISTIAN HOPE

8:18:	the coming glory to be revealed unto us
8:19:	the revelation of the sons of God
8:21:	the glorious freedom of the children of God
8:23:	sonship . . . the redemption of our body
8:25:	that which we do not yet see
8:28:	the good
8:32:	ALL THINGS

b. We justified Christians have the sure hope that no one will condemn us because Christ intercedes for us with God.

8:33 Any possible answer that could be offered to the bold question of "who will bring a charge against God's elected ones?" Paul supersedes with the resounding protestation that "it is God who justifies." Indeed, God's "elected ones," we Christians, have already been unequivocally "justified" by God (3:21–26; 5:1–11; etc.), so that we stand clearly acquitted before any tribunal or judgment seat. And, since in the last analysis it would be the charge or condemnation of God himself that would really matter, it is all the more certain that no one can really bring a charge against us.

8:34 Paul likewise convinces his audience that there is no one who can possibly condemn us, because Christ himself, who died and was raised by God, now sits in a privileged position at the right hand of God interceding "for us!"

With irrefutable argumentation Paul reassuringly convinces us Christians of the certainty of our hope that God *will give* us "all things," the totality of his future salvation, not only because God clearly shows that he is wholly "for us" in the *past* death of his Son "for us," but also because Christ *presently* intercedes at the right hand of God "for us."

Paul eloquently elevates his readers to the pinnacle of complete certainty and absolute assurance regarding their hope for future triumph over present distress, based on the magnificence of God's tremendous love:

6. *Romans 8:35–39:*

35 Who will separate us from the love of Christ? Suffering, or distress, or persecution, or famine, or destitution, or danger, or sword? 36 It stands written:

> "For your sake we are being put to death all the day long;
> we are regarded as sheep for slaughter" (Ps 44:22).

37 But in all these things we are more than triumphing through him who loved us. 38 For I am convinced that neither death nor life, neither angels nor demons, neither things present nor things to come, not spiritual powers, 39 neither height nor depth, nor any other creature will be able to separate us from the love of God in Christ Jesus our Lord!

a. *Nothing has the power to separate suffering Christians from the love of Christ.*

8:35 As Paul has previously proclaimed, the "love of Christ" refers to God's unique love for us as manifested in Christ's dying for us while we were still sinners (5:8). This is the same splendid love of God that has been profusely poured into our inner beings, our "hearts," through the Holy Spirit that was given to us; and the same love that assures that our hope does not shame us (5:5).

Since the "love of Christ" consists in his *death* on our behalf, with clever perceptiveness Paul forces his audience to realize that our present tribulations and problems, even if they result in our death, can never separate us from the extraordinary love of Christ.

8:36 Indeed, the rhetorically powerful accumulation of afflictions experienced by Paul and his fellow Christians—suffering, distress, persecution, famine, destitution, danger, sword—are all summed up and authoritatively interpreted by the holy scripture of Psalm 44:22 as a "being put to death," a sacrificial "slaughter," for "your sake," for the sake of God rather than for any guilt on our part.

Since all our many adversities are tantamount to our "death" *for the sake of God,* they surely cannot separate us from the love of Christ, which is his *death* for us; on the contrary, they can only unite us ever closer to that death and love! Paul's listeners are thus consoled, comforted and encouraged to face their daily hardships with a refreshed and renewed hope.

b. We Christians are absolutely assured of final triumph through the love of God in Christ Jesus.

8:37 As Paul energetically exclaims, in the midst of all these trials and tribulations that we Christians continually undergo, we are "more than triumphing," that is, we are confidently and triumphantly marching on our way to the future, final victory of the God who loved us in the death of Christ.

8:38–39 Paul reinforces his audience's sure hope of attaining God's magnificent, final triumph with his own authoritative and personal "conviction" that *nothing will ever be able, will ever have the "power,"* to separate us from the tremendously powerful love of God in Christ.

Here Paul boldly and brashly broadens the horizon of our Christian hope to utter extremes. Not only our present sufferings (8:18, 35) and our "being put to death" (8:36) but any of the mutually opposing and all-encompassing apocalyptic powers dominant within the whole universe and all of creation—death or life, angels or demons, things now present or things to come, spiritual powers, height or depth, or *any other creature!*—will ever possess enough power to separate us from the firm foundation of our hope for God's final and triumphant victory, namely, the phenomenally powerful love of God manifested in Christ's death on our behalf.

With this dramatic delineation of all possible powers that can embrace human existence, Paul puts the final, climactic touch on his concerted effort to convince his audience of the complete and absolute assurance of their hope that the coming glory to be revealed to us Christians will far exceed our present sufferings (8:18)!

OUR FINAL TRIUMPH THROUGH GOD'S LOVE

. . . we are *more than triumphing* through him who *loved* us (8:37).
For I am *convinced* that
neither death nor life,
neither angels nor demons,
neither things present nor things to come,
not spiritual powers,
neither height nor depth,
nor ANY OTHER CREATURE
will be able to separate
us from the *love* of God in Christ Jesus our Lord! (8:38–39).

I. Summary

With exhilarating encouragement Paul has invited his readers and all Christians to join him in boldly and confidently proclaiming the hope that is integral to and consequent upon our having been justified by faith through the death of Christ (5:1–11).

Then with dramatically pointed comparisons and contrasts he reassured and consoled his audience with the realism of this hope: It is precisely in the midst of the ever-present, debilitating powers of sin and death that we Christians may claim and cling to the sure hope for God's future eternal life, a hope that more than replaces and far exceeds the hopelessness of sin and death (5:12–21).

He persuasively prodded his listeners to actualize the possibility to live already, as part of our hope, the future life for which we hope (6:1–14). Indeed, he persistently urged that they *must* live this hope now; it is more than a mere possibility, it is a necessity; otherwise they risk a return to utter despair (6:15–23).

Focusing upon the role of God's Law, Paul presented a further reason why we can and must live out hope now: we have already been liberated from dismal hopelessness under the realm of the Law (7:1–6).

Paul then required his readers to empathize and commiserate with the common predicament of every individual human being who is helplessly mangled from within by the pervasive and permeating powers of sin and death, which have deceitfully transformed the good Law of God into a "Law" of sin leading only to the desperate finality of death (7:7–25).

But he revitalized the downcast spirits of his listeners with an exuberant proclamation that for us Christians who are joined to Christ Jesus through baptism there is now a "Law" of the Spirit of life which assures our hope for God's future, final life (8:1–17).

Finally, with an electrifying, climactic surge Paul invited his audience and all Christians to join in his enthusiastic enunciations of the utterly unsurpassed magnificence and absolute assurance of our Christian hope of participating in God's final, triumphant victory over all our ever-present tribulations and over all the menacing powers of evil (8:18–39).

NOTES

1. A rhetorical "gradatio" or progression is a continuing repetition in which the last member of a syntactical group is repeated as the first member

of the following group. This chain-like repetition emphatically raises the expression from one level to the next, and often, as here, further explains the expression. The "gradatio" in Rom 5:3–4 exemplifies the "modus per incrementa" in which the most stressed member of the series, in this case, "hope," is placed in the final emphatic position. See H. Lausberg, *Handbuch der Literarischen Rhetorik* (2d ed.; Munich: Hueber, 1973) #619, 623, 653, 451.

2. There are several passages elsewhere in Paul where "steadfastness" is closely associated with and further describes the attitude of "hope" in the midst of opposition and suffering: 1 Cor 13:7; 2 Cor 1:6–7; 6:4; 12:12: 1 Thes 1:3.

3. "Heart" (*kardia*) refers to the inner life of a person, to the "core" of one's being; it is "the source or seat of all the forces and functions of soul and spirit." See J. Behm, "*kardia*," *TDNT* 3 (1965) 611.

4. This "how much more then" type of *qal wahomer* conclusion exemplifies the first exegetical rule of Rabbi Hillel; see Str-B, 3. 223–226.

5. On the concept of "reconciliation" in Paul, see J. A. Fitzmyer, "Reconciliation in Pauline Theology," *To Advance the Gospel. New Testament Studies* (New York: Crossroad, 1981) 162–185; R. P. Martin, *Reconciliation. A Study of Paul's Theology* (New Foundations Theological Library; Atlanta: Knox, 1981) 140–154; O. Hofius, "Erwägungen zur Gestalt und Herkunft des paulinischen Versöhnungsgedankens," *ZTK* 77 (1980) 186–199.

6. There is quite possibly an allusion here to the primeval situation of human beings as represented in the story of Adam and Eve. See Gen 2—3, especially 2:16–17.

7. A figurative use of "law" (*nomos*) in the sense of "rule" or "regularity," but retaining an allusion to the Mosaic Law, which can also have this connotation. Hence, the word "law" here conveys a certain ambivalence or "double-duty" character.

8. Another figurative use of "law" (*nomos*), this time with the connotation of an active force or power, but still retaining a reference to the Mosaic Law.

9. Despite the alleged problem of this final repetition of despair coming immediately after the thanksgiving in 7:25, we find no convincing reason to regard it as a gloss, since it can be satisfactorily interpreted in relation to 7:14–23. See C. E. B. Cranfield, *A Critical and Exegetical Commentary on the Epistle to the Romans* (ICC; 2 vols.; Edinburgh: T. & T. Clark, 1975, 1979) 368.

10. Another figurative use of "law" (*nomos*) but in reference to the Torah as God's instructions, directives and right order for living.

11. This "likeness" includes both an identity and a non-identity to the sinful human condition: it is not an identity insofar as Christ was God's own (sinless) Son, but it is more than a mere superficial resemblance insofar as Christ was truly and fully human.

12. "Abba" is the Aramaic word for "father."

13. Paul combines "eager expectation" (*apokaradokia*) and "await" (*apekdechetai*) elsewhere to likewise express the intense expectation and eagerness of our Christian hope: 1 Cor 1:7; Phil 1:20; 3:20; Gal 5:5.

14. The reference to "groaning" for the future heavenly dwelling of God in 2 Cor 5:2, 4 is similar to the "groaning" in Rom 8:23; and there is a similar function for the Spirit—a "guarantee" of future glory in 2 Cor 5:5 and the "first-fruits" of future glory in Rom 8:23.

15. On the "striving" of the Spirit, see Rom 8:5–7; in 8:6 the "striving" of the Spirit is toward eschatological "life and peace."

Chapter VI

Romans 9:1–11:36

A. Rom 9:1–5: Paul Shares with His Audience His Deep Concern for His Fellow Israelites Who Do Not Yet Believe in Jesus Christ.

In Romans 1–8 Paul has constructed a concerted and coherent presentation of the gospel designed to convince his readers and all Christians of the marvelous benefits they now have as believers in Jesus Christ. He has thereby made great strides toward achieving his stated purpose of spiritually strengthening and encouraging his audience through the faith they have in common with Paul (1:11–12). With a definite shift of tone and theme in Romans 9–11 Paul begins another concerted and coherent thrust intended to have a persuasive impact upon his listeners.

Although a literary unity in itself, Romans 9–11 is by no means merely an excursus unrelated to Paul's previous proclamation of the gospel in Romans 1–8. The gnawing problem that Paul addresses in Romans 9–11 looms as a most crucial one not only for Paul personally but for all Christians. It is the perturbing enigma of why most of the people of Israel, God's uniquely chosen people, do not believe in the gospel about the Christ who has come "according to the flesh" (1:3; 9:5) from Israel.

Indeed, Paul previously announced the gospel to be the "power of God for salvation for all who believe, *for the Jew first* and also for the Greek" (1:16). The failure of most Jews to believe therefore calls into question for Paul and all Christians the power of the gospel, as God's efficacious word, to be the valid basis for all the benefits Paul has claimed for believers throughout Romans 1–8.

In other words, if the powerful word of God has not brought Is-

rael as God's people to faith in their own Messiah, how firmly can
Christians rest their faith and hope upon God's word in the gospel
about his Son? What role does Israel's glaring failure to believe play in
God's purpose and plan for salvation? How are Christians to look
upon and relate to the Jews who have not believed in Christ? These
are critical questions Paul engages his readers to grapple with in Romans 9–11.

With regard to its literary-rhetorical style, Romans 9–11 exhibits
a distinctive character. Paul continues to employ the diatribal, dial-
ogic manner of argumentation, fully exploiting the device of rhetorical statements and interrogations addressed to an imaginary
interlocutor.

But Paul pursues his argumentation largely through the vehicle
of an intriguing assortment of explicit scriptural quotations, woven
together according to a pattern of key words and associated themes.
This preponderance of scriptural citations, authoritatively repre-
senting God's recorded will and plan for salvation, appears as most
appropriate to the major thesis of Paul's argument, namely, that
"the word of God has not failed" (9:6). Paul skillfully and astutely
utilizes the very "word of God" to convincingly prove that indeed
"the word of God has not failed" either with regard to Israel or
Christians.[1]

With candid and frank sincerity Paul divulges his deep personal
pain and concern for his fellow Israelites who have not believed in
Christ:

1. Romans 9:1–5:

1 I tell the truth in Christ, I do not lie, as my conscience bears me
witness in the Holy Spirit, 2 that my sorrow is great and I have continual anguish in my heart. 3 For I could pray that I myself be accursedly
separated from Christ for the sake of my brothers, my kinsfolk by
race. 4 They are Israelites, to whom belong the sonship and the glory
and the covenants and the giving of the Law and the worship and the
promises, 5 to whom belong the patriarchs and from whom is the
Christ according to the flesh who is over all, God be blessed for ever,
Amen!

a. Paul has a most serious solicitude for his fellow Israelites.

9:1–2 Paul emphatically reinforces the positive assertion that "I
tell the truth in Christ" with its negative counterpart, "I do not lie," to
insistently impress upon his audience the profound seriousness of

what he is about to communicate to them. It is an intense seriousness honestly spoken "in Christ" and confirmed in his conscience by the "Holy Spirit." He wants his listeners to sense the severe sorrow and incessant agony he harbors within his heart for the people of Israel.

9:3 And so Paul jolts his readers with a startling intercessory prayer: So passionate is his concern for his fellow Israelites that he would go so far as to sacrifice his own adherence to Christ and thus exchange places with unbelieving Israel, if that were possible, for the sake of bringing his kinsfolk to faith in Christ.[2] With this obviously impossible but sincerely intended prayer-wish Paul shares his ardent solicitude and resolute regard for Israel with his auditors. And so they must also be deeply concerned.

b. God gave the Israelites many privileges and prerogatives including the Christ.

9:4–5 Paul displays the reason for this reverent respect by summoning his readers' attention to the striking array of genuine privileges bequeathed to the people of Israel by God: First of all, they are privileged to be known by their divinely designated name of "Israel" (see Gen 32:28).

They are "Israelites" and as "Israelites" they possess such salvation-historical prerogatives as the familial relation of "sonship" with God their Father (see Exod 4:22; Deut 14:1–2; Hos 11:1; Jer 31:9), the "glory" of God's closeness and presence (see Exod 16:10; 24:16–17; 40:34–35), the various "covenants" pledged to them by God (see Gen 6:18; 9:9; 15:18; 17:1–14, 19; Exod 2:24; Sir 44:12, 18–23; Wis 18:22; 2 Macc 8:15), the gift of God's Law (see Exod 20:1–17; Deut 5:1–21), the "worship" of God in his Temple, the "promises" for future salvation (see Rom 4:13–20), the "patriarchs" (Abraham, Isaac, Jacob, etc.) to whom God granted the covenants and the promises.

But most of all, by way of climax to all these privileges, Paul will not have his audience forget that it is from the "Israelites" that the Messiah, "the Christ" came with regard to his human descent (see Rom 1:3). Paul accentuates the eminence of this climactic prerogative with a sudden and fervent outburst of grateful praise to God for the unsurpassed gift of his Messiah (see Rom 1:25).[3]

Despite this stunning list of God-given privileges and blessings afforded the "Israelites," the sad fact painfully persists for Paul, his readers and all his fellow Christians that the people of Israel as a whole have not believed in God's gospel about the Christ.

B. Rom 9:6–29: But the Word of God Has Not Failed With Regard to Israel.

Paul commences a brilliantly and carefully crafted scriptural argumentation aimed at illustrating and proving for his readers how God's purpose and plan has always been and still is operative with regard to Israel.

1. Romans 9:6–9:

6 But it is not as if the word of God has failed! For not all the descendants of Israel are actually "Israel." 7 Nor are all the children (of Abraham) the "seed" of Abraham, but, "through Isaac there will be called a seed for you" (Gen 21:12). 8 This means that it is not the children of the flesh that are the children of God, but the children of the promise are reckoned as "seed." 9 For this is the word of the promise: "At this time I will return and Sarah will have a son" (Gen 18:10, 14).

a. The powerful and promising word of God has not at all failed.

9:6 Lest his listeners entertain any thoughts that perhaps the "word of God" has proved to be impotent or actually abandoned the people of Israel, in view of the fact that they have refused to believe in the Messiah that originates from them, Paul vehemently insists that in no way has the word of God "failed" or "fallen away."[4]

That the "word of God has (indeed) not failed" functions as the thesis statement or superscription for the intriguing argumentation that follows. It is of immense importance for Paul and all of his fellow Christians. For if the word of God has failed with regard to Israel, can this same word of God in the gospel constitute a truly trustworthy foundation for Christian faith and hope?

b. God's word of promise worked through the election of Isaac as a descendant of Abraham.

9:6–7 The effectiveness of God's word is clearly evident, as Paul maintains, in the way that it works through the principle of God's free choice or election. God's election is apparent in his choice of the family line of Isaac rather than of Ishmael (see Gen 21:8–14) to inherit and carry on the promise that accompanies designation as the special "seed" (descendants) of Abraham.

For not all those who are actually descendants of Israel comprise the "Israel" through whom the word of God's powerful promise continues to operate. Nor are all the children of Abraham designated as the privileged "seed" of Abraham, but as the scriptural word of God's promise itself verifies in Gen 21:12, it is through *Isaac* (not Ishmael or anyone else) that "there will be called a seed for you."

9:8 In other words, it is not physical descent from Abraham that instates the children of Abraham as the children of God, but it is the very *promise* of God that installs them as "the children of the promise" who are thereby "reckoned" or "counted" by God as the prestigious "seed" of Abraham.

9:9 As the scriptural "word of the promise" itself certifies, God bestowed upon Sarah as opposed to Hagar the promise of bearing a son (Gen 18:10, 14).

And so Paul has begun to lead his readers to an acknowledgment that the word of God has not in fact failed (9:6), but has operated through election, as evident in his election of Sarah and Isaac over Hagar and Ishmael for the promise of being the privileged "seed" of Abraham and the "children of God."

2. *Romans 9:10–13:*

10 Not only that, but also when Rebecca conceived children by one man, Isaac our father, 11 even though they were not yet born nor had done anything either good or bad, in order that the purpose of God might continue according to election, 12 not from works but from the One who calls, she was told, "The elder will serve the younger" (Gen 25:23). 13 As it is written, "Jacob I loved, but Esau I hated" (Mal 1:2–3).

a. God freely chose Jacob over his twin brother Esau.

9:10 Paul advances to the next generation of patriarchs and matriarchs in his scriptural argumentation to illustrate how God's election is even more graphically manifested by his choosing of Jacob over his older brother Esau. Both Jacob and Esau were conceived through one and the same act of conception between Rebecca and Isaac, so that they were full, twin brothers with the same mother, unlike the half brothers Isaac and Ishmael.

b. The purpose of God perdures by his free election and calling.

9:11–12 But even before they were born and so before they were able to do anything either good or bad, Rebecca was issued God's promise indicating his election of Jacob over Esau: "The elder (Esau) will serve the younger (Jacob)" (Gen 25:23).

9:13 And this is further confirmed by the more explicit scriptural statement of God's free choice: "Jacob I loved, but Esau I hated" (Mal 1:2–3).

All of this illustrates how the salvific purpose of God proceeds strictly according to the principle of his free election, and so not on the merit of anyone's performance of works, but solely from the "One who calls."

Paul continues to shape his audience's attitude toward God and his powerful word by inducing them to realize that "the word of God has not failed" (9:6); on the contrary, the purpose of God persists, but it persists in accord with the free choice of the God "who calls" (9:11–12).

3. Romans 9:14–18:

14 What shall we say then? Is there injustice here from the side of God? By no means! 15 For he says to Moses, "I will have mercy on whom I have mercy, and I will have compassion on whom I have compassion" (Exod 33:19). 16 So then (the purpose of God depends)[5] not upon anyone's willing nor upon anyone's striving, but upon God's showing of mercy. 17 For the scripture says to Pharaoh, "For this very purpose I have raised you up, in order that I might show my power in you, and in order that my name might be proclaimed in all the earth" (Exod 9:16). 18 So then he has mercy on whomever he wills, and he hardens whomever he wills.

a. In his absolute sovereignty God remains true to himself.

9:14 With a return to a diatribal type of questioning Paul entices his listeners to consider, in light of the foregoing examples of God's free election (9:6–13), whether there might perhaps be detected some "injustice" here on the part of God. But Paul abruptly discards any such misconception from the mind of his audience with a resounding "By no means!"

9:15 With the aid of the recorded word of God Paul firmly asserts that in his absolute freedom and sovereignty God remains totally true and faithful to himself, for he himself, with emphatic insistence upon his own sovereignty, proclaims to Moses that "*I* will have mercy on whom *I* have mercy, and *I* will have compassion on whom *I* have compassion" (Exod 33:19).

b. God's purpose persists solely according to his own will.

9:16 This further explains how the salvific "purpose of God" proceeds according to election (9:11) and does not depend upon any human "willing" or "striving," but solely upon the absolutely sovereign God's "showing of mercy."

Paul has thus aroused in his readership an attitude of profound and reverent awe toward the totally sovereign God, an awe tinted with an inkling of gratitude for the mercy of God.

9:17 As he progresses with his scriptural demonstration, Paul startles his listeners: Not only does God advance his salvific purpose according to election by having "mercy" on whomever he "wills" (e.g. on Moses in Exod 33:17–19), but he can even carry out his plan by "hardening" (the heart) of whomever he "wills" (e.g. Pharaoh in Exod 4:21; 7:3; 9:12; 10:20; 11:10; 14:4, 17)! For in his address to Pharaoh God himself emphatically affirms his complete and ultimate control of his own plan: "For this very purpose *I* have raised you up, in order that *I* might show *my power* in you, and in order that *my name* might be proclaimed in all the earth" (Exod 9:16).

The manifestation of the "power" of God (by saving the people of Israel in the Exodus event) and the proclamation of the "name" of God throughout the world furthers his salvific plan (9:11) and fulfills his word (9:6) even through the "hardening," the negative aspect of his free election.

9:18 Paul will have his readership realize, then, that not only through "mercy" but also through "hardening" God accomplishes his salvific purpose because of his sovereign "will."

Furthermore, he has shrewdly induced his audience to perceive a similarity between the "hardening" of the heart of Pharaoh and the hardened hearts of presently unbelieving Israel in the overall salvific plan of God.

Paul shifts to the next phase of his well crafted argumentation by short-circuiting a potential objection to his provocative reasoning:

4. Romans 9:19–21:

19 You will say to me then, "What fault can he still find? For who can resist his will?" 20 O (mere) human being, who are you to answer back to God? Will what is molded say to the molder, "Why have you made me thus?" 21 Or does not the potter have authority over the clay, to make from the same lump one vessel for honor and another for dishonor?

a. No one should question God's sovereign will.

9:19 Through the diatribal device of dialoguing with an imaginary partner, Paul raises an objection to his argument: How would it be possible for God to still find fault with anyone (in the judgment), if no one can really resist his sovereign "will"? In other words, what can anyone do that does not in some way serve God's plan? Even those who seem to resist it (like Pharaoh) actually obey it!

b. God has the absolute authority to fashion his creatures in accord with his own purpose.

9:20–21 But Paul flatly overrules this objection with keen counter-questions derived from traditional biblical imagery in which the absolute authority that God as creator exercises over his creatures is quite appropriately compared to the complete power that a potter possesses over his clay (see Isa 29:16; 45:9; 64:7; Wis 15:7; Jer 18:6; Job 10:9; 33:6; Sir 33:10–13). How can a mere human being even dare to question the creative designs of his sovereign creator, who, like a potter, can fashion and form his own creatures in any way he wishes?

Paul thus causes his listeners to concede that God as sovereign creator has the "authority," the right or freedom of choice, to make his creatures serve different functions in the accomplishment of his salvific purpose. He has cleverly directed his audience toward recognizing that, although their respective roles differ, both Christians and unbelieving Israel have definite and essential parts to play in the unfolding of God's salvific plan:

5. Romans 9:22–26:

22 But what if God, willing to manifest his wrath and to make known his power, has endured with much patience vessels of wrath designed for destruction, 23 and in order to make known the wealth of his glory upon vessels of mercy, which he has prepared beforehand for glory . . . ? 24 We are those whom he thus called not only from the Jews but also from the Gentiles, 25 as indeed he says in Hosea:

"I will call what was not my people 'my people'
and her who was not beloved 'beloved'.
And it will be in the place where it was said to them,
'You are not my people,'
there they will be called sons of the living God." (Hos 2:25, 1).

a. God has endured with much patience the Israelites he created as "vessels of wrath."

9:22 Further playing upon the God as potter imagery, Paul shares with his readers a perceptive and revealing insight into God's sovereign plan. He now clearly draws out the implications of his earlier reference to Pharaoh's role in God's salvific design. Much like Pharaoh in the Exodus event, presently unbelieving Israel plays the role of the "vessels of wrath" in God's salvific purpose.

It was God's free and sovereign "will" to "harden" the heart of Pharaoh and thereby advance his salvific aim by dramatically *"manifesting"* his *"power"* through Pharaoh for the sake of saving the people of God by leading them out of Egypt in the Exodus event so that the "name" of God might be spread throughout all the earth (9:17). Similarly, it is now God's sovereign "will" to save his people by *"manifesting"* his wrath and making known his *"power"* in enduring with much patience "vessels of wrath," unbelieving Israel, fit for destruction.

God's manifestation of his wrath and power in unbelieving Israel promotes his salvific intention, since it is oriented to the salvation of those who have been "called" to future glory as "vessels of mercy," namely, believing Christians as the reconstituted people of God. The negative role played by unbelieving Israel as "vessels of wrath" suitable only for destruction has its positive counterpart within God's overall salvific scheme in the role assumed by believing Christians as "vessels of mercy" shaped for God's future "glory".

This poignantly illustrates how God, the Potter who freely crafted his own creation, fashions one vessel for the role of "honor" and another for "dishonor" (9:21). Paul is causing his readership to realize that the disturbing situation of unbelieving Israel does not in fact destroy but actually furthers God's salvific strategy (9:11), so that the powerful word of God has not failed (9:6).

And he has aroused at least a faint glimmer of hope for unbelieving Israel herself, indicated by the expression of God's "enduring" them "with much patience," as such enduring patience is intended to bring them to conversion (see Rom 2:4).

b. God prepared Christians as "vessels of mercy" for the wealth of his glory.

9:23 Closely coordinated to the "vessels of wrath" within God's sovereign design are the "vessels of mercy," that is, believing Christians. These "vessels of mercy" illustrate how the salvific plan of God persists even now by the free and sovereign election of the God who "calls" and "shows mercy" (9:6–21). It is part of God's salvific will to make known the great wealth of his glory upon vessels of mercy, which he prepared beforehand for future glory.

9:24 And "we" Christians are the ones whom God has already "called," not only from the Jews but also from the Gentiles, to be vessels of his "mercy."

9:25–26 Our having been "called" by God fulfills God's word of promise as recorded by the prophet Hosea (Hos 2:25 and 2:1 in the Hebrew text), according to which God would "call" forth a new people and bestow upon them the privilege of being "called" the sons of the living God.

We Christians represent this new people of God composed of Jews and Gentiles, graciously entitled to be "called" sons of God. Paul thus inserts our "calling" as Christians into the free and sovereign election of the God who "calls":

CHRISTIANS AND THE GOD WHO "CALLS"

9:7:   "through Isaac there will be *called* a seed for you" (Gen 21:12).

9:11–
12:       . . . that the purpose of God might continue according to election, not from works but from the One who *calls* . . .

9:24:   We are those whom he thus *called* . . .

9:25:   "I will *call* what was not my people 'my people' . . .

9:26:   there they will be *called* sons of the living God" (Hos 2:25, 1).

By the very fact that we Christians are the ones toward whom God has shown his "mercy" (9:15–18, 23) and "called" to be a new people and sons of God from both Jews and Gentiles, Paul has soothingly reassured his audience that, despite Israel's failure to believe, the firm word of God's promise (9:6, 25–26) and his continuing salvific purpose (9:11) have not at all failed but still stand as a stalwart foundation for Christian faith and hope.

But what about the future of *unbelieving* Israel, Paul's primary concern and worry here (9:1–5)? Does the word of God still stand for Israel? Indeed! For with enthusiastic delight Paul presents the prophetic promise for the future of Israel as pronounced by the prophet Isaiah:

6. Romans 9:27–29:

27 And Isaiah cries out on behalf of Israel: "If the number of the sons of Israel be as the sand of the sea, a remnant will be saved! 28 For, fully completing and firmly establishing (it), the Lord will execute (his) word (of promise) on the earth!" (Isa 10:22–23; Hos 2:1). 29 And as Isaiah has foretold: "If the Lord of hosts had not left us a seed, we

would have become as Sodom and we would have been made like Gomorrah" (Isa 1:9).

a. God's prophetic promise stirs the hope that surely at least a remnant will be saved from the many sons of Israel.

9:27 Through the prophetic "crying out" of Isaiah on Israel's behalf Paul demonstrates that there is still a hopeful word of God for unbelieving Israel. The hope that a "remnant" of Israel "*will be saved*" is based upon God's word of promise to Abraham that his descendants would be as numerous "as the sand of the sea" (Gen 22:17; 32:9–12).

In other words, if the number of (still unbelieving) Israel[6] is to be as numerous as the sand of the sea in accord with God's "word" of promise, which is still operative and effective (9:6, 28), then surely at least a remnant of unbelieving Israel will be saved.[7] Thus, there is hope that at least some of the unbelieving Israelites, the "vessels of wrath designed for destruction" (9:22), will believe and be saved by God.

9:28 The second part of Isaiah's "cry" injects added certainty into the hope that "a remnant will be saved" by assuring that God will ultimately fulfill his "word" (9:6, 28) of promise and surely bring his salvific "purpose" (9:11) to its final and decisive conclusion on earth.

b. God's promise of a remnant presents the hope that Israel will not undergo total and final annihilation.

9:29 Paul then presents yet further hope for Israel by citing another prophetic passage (Isa 1:9) which applies to Israel's present situation. That which the prophet Isaiah has foretold can now be spoken by unbelieving Israel, as the hope represented by a "remnant" is taken up and developed by the hope represented by a "seed" which God has left for "us," namely unbelieving Israelites. If God had not left for "*us*" a seed, then "*we*" (unbelieving Israel) would have been totally without hope because "*we*" would have been utterly destroyed like the infamous cities of Sodom and Gomorrah (Gen 19:24–29).

There is an added aspect to the hope for unbelieving Israel here. Whereas Paul previously voiced the sure hope that at least a remnant will be saved from the promised great number of Israelites (9:27–28), he now expresses the hope that this remnant or seed implies for the non-remnant remainder of unbelieving Israel. In other words, unbelieving Israelites, the "we" who are now the speakers of what was prophetically foretold, hold to the hope that "we" will not suffer final destruction like Sodom and Gomorrah because God has promised to leave "us" a seed or remnant. The hope for a remnant (9:27–28) thus implies and includes a hope for the others as well.

Not only has Paul reinforced the faith and hope of his Christian readers, both Jews and Gentiles (9:24), in the unfailing word of God despite the failure of Israel to believe (9:22–26), but he has also ignited a spark of hope within his audience for unbelieving Israel, a hope based upon the still effective word (9:6, 27–29) and the still continuing salvific purpose of God (9:11).

C. Rom 9:30–10:21: Faith Is Still Available to Israel.

Paul now shifts the vantage point of his argument. Whereas he previously invited his readership to consider the problem of unbelieving Israel primarily from the side of God (9:6–29), he now bids them to ponder the same problem primarily from the side of Israel.

1. Romans 9:30–33:

30 What then shall we say? Gentiles who did not pursue righteousness have attained righteousness, the righteousness (that comes) from faith; 31 but Israel who pursued the Law of righteousness did not arrive at the Law! 32 Why? Because (they sought to attain it) not from faith but as if (it could be attained) by works. They stumbled over the stone of stumbling, 33 as it is written, "Behold, I place in Zion a stone of stumbling and rock of offense, but the one who believes in him will not be put to shame" (Isa 28:16).

a. Gentiles have ironically attained the very righteousness Israel mistakenly pursued by doing works of the law.

9:30–31 Continuing his diatribal dialogue Paul fixes his audience's attention upon the ironical paradox of Israel's unbelief. Although the people of Israel have long struggled and strained to achieve the right relationship with God that the Mosaic Law intends and promises, they have fallen miserably short of that goal, while the Gentiles who did not even seek such "righteousness" have quite amazingly attained it!

9:32 Israel failed to gain "righteousness" because they have mistakenly attempted to accomplish it by performing the works of the Law rather than by believing in Christ. In other words, Israel has not realized that God's "righteousness" is now available through faith in Christ and not through the doing of the works of the Law (see Rom 3:20–22).

b. Israel has stumbled over Christ but may still believe in him.

9:32–33 With the aid of the scriptural word of God, Paul interprets this failure of Israel as a "stumbling over the stone of stumbling." The people of Israel have "stumbled over" the very "stone" which, as recorded in Isa 28:16, God himself placed in Zion (Israel) as the new means of attaining righteousness. This "stone," of course, refers to Christ (see 10:11) and there is added irony in the fact that God himself placed this "stone" in the midst of Israel.

But although this "stone" has caused Israel to "stumble" and take "offense," their stumbling is not necessarily a definitive fall (see 11:11). The scriptural quote of God's word ends on a note of persistent promise and appeal. It may well be that the people of Israel have stumbled over Christ, the "stone," *but* there is always available to them the hopeful pledge that "whoever *believes* in him will not be put to shame." Although Israel "has stumbled" in not attaining righteousness from faith, the hope that they "will not be put to shame"[8] by God in the final judgment is still accessible to them in accord with God's own word of promise, if they only *believe* in Christ.

Although Israel has only to believe to be saved, the distressing fact that they have not believed lingers. Paul turns directly to his audience with his ardent and heartfelt concern for unbelieving Israel:

2. *Romans 10:1–4:*

1 Brothers, my heart's desire and prayer to God for them is for their salvation. 2 I testify on their behalf that they have a zeal for God, but it is not directed by knowledge. 3 For, failing to recognize God's righteousness and seeking to establish their own righteousness, they have not submitted to the righteousness of God. 4 For Christ is the end of the Law, so that righteousness comes to all who believe.

a. Paul ardently prays for the salvation of Israelites who have a zeal for but not the proper knowledge of God.

10:1–2 Continuing to confide to his readers his deep personal solicitude and prayers to God that his fellow Israelites arrive at salvation (see 9:1–3), Paul puts his finger on the crux of Israel's problem. Although, to their credit, they have a burning zeal for God, it is unfortunately defective because it is not directed by the proper knowledge of what God has now brought about.

b. In seeking their own righteousness by the Law Israelites have failed to recognize the righteousness of God by faith in Christ.

10:3 In tenaciously striving to establish their own relation of righteousness with God by performing the works of the Law, they have refused to acknowledge and humbly submit themselves in faith to the new "righteousness of God."

10:4 For, as Paul would have his Christian readers realize, Christ has now brought about the definite "end," the termination, of the Law as the means through which one attains righteousness with God.[9] Righteousness now comes to all who *believe,* rather than to those who zealously seek to gain it by doing the works of the Law.

With further reference to scripture Paul continues to convince his listeners that the righteousness based on doing the works of the Law has now been terminated by God's righteousness based on faith in Christ:

3. Romans 10:5–8:

5 For Moses writes about the righteousness that comes from the Law: "The person who does them (the works or commandments of the Law) will live by them" (Lev 18:5). 6 But the righteousness that comes from faith speaks thus, "Do not say in your heart (see Deut 9:4), Who will ascend into heaven?" (see Deut 30:12), that is, to bring Christ down; 7 or "Who will descend into the abyss?" (see Deut 30:13), that is, to bring Christ up from the dead. 8 But what does it say?—"The word is near you, in your mouth and in your heart" (see Deut 30:14), that is, the word of faith which we preach.

a. Those who seek righteousness from the Law must live by doing the works of the Law.

10:5 Shrewdly and appropriately calling upon the very words of the Torah, Paul perceptively points out how Moses himself issued a warning that in the righteousness based on the Law a person must "live" and so sustain his/her life by "doing" the works and keeping the commandments of the Law. In other words, under the Law a person gains "life" only if he/she is able to perform the works and commandments of the Law. Since Paul has already demonstrated how all have miserably failed to keep the Law (3:9, 19–20, 23), the attaining of righteousness through the Law has come to an end. No one can "live" by doing the commandments.

b. But in righteousness from faith the word of faith is very close to all.

10:6–7 With astute cleverness Paul concocts a stunning reinterpretation of a Torah text from Deuteronomy 30:12–14, in which he unabashedly steals statements about the marvelous nearness to Israel of God's word in the Law and transfers them to Christ and the word of faith in Christ. This further illustrates how Christ is the "end" or termination of the Law (10:4).

Israel of old delighted in the fact that the commandments of God's Law or Torah were so close to them that no one had to "ascend into heaven" in order to bring them down or "descend into the abyss" in order to bring them up. God spoke them directly through Moses on Mount Sinai.

But according to the new righteousness that now comes from faith and not from the Law, it is Christ who is so wonderfully near to all who believe. No one had to ascend to heaven to bring Christ down and no one had to descend into the abyss to bring him up, for God himself has already brought him from heaven and raised him from the dead.

10:8 Therefore, no longer is it the word of the Law that is so near to each individual so that it is in one's very heart and mouth, but now it is the "word of faith" which "we" (Paul and his co-workers) preach that is so very close to each and every individual. As Deuteronomy 30:14, with heavy accentuation upon the *nearness* of the "word" of faith to each and every person, aptly proclaims: "The word is *near you,* in *your* mouth and in *your* heart."[10] And this "word" is the preached "word" of the gospel which instigates and leads to "faith."

Paul wants his readers to grasp, agree and verify that God has brought faith so near to all that it is readily available to each and every individual, including, and most especially, unbelieving Israelites.

Paul draws out the implications of the nearness of the word of faith so that it is in one's very "mouth" and "heart":

4. Romans 10:9–13:

9 If you confess with your mouth that Jesus is Lord and believe in your heart that God raised him from the dead, you will be saved. 10 For with the heart a person believes for righteousness, and with the mouth a person confesses for salvation. 11 As scripture says, "Everyone who believes in him will not be put to shame" (Isa 28:16). 12 For there is no distinction between Jew and Greek; the same

Lord is Lord of all, bestowing riches upon all who call upon him. 13 For "everyone who calls upon the name of the Lord will be saved!" (Joel 3:5).

a. Each individual must only believe to have the sure hope for salvation.

10:9 Further developing the idea of the innermost nearness of the word of faith to the individual in Deuteronomy 30:14, Paul adeptly illustrates the hope that results when one believes. So close is the preached word of faith to one's mouth and heart, that "you," the individual person, must only open your mouth and acknowledge the supreme lordship of Jesus and allow your heart, your inmost being, to accept in faith that God raised him from the dead and then "you" will possess the secure hope that "you will be saved!"

10:10 For with the heart a person believes and thus has hope for future, eschatological "righteousness," and with the mouth a person confesses and thus has hope for future, eschatological "salvation." This "salvation" which is the goal of Christian hope is precisely the "salvation" (10:1) Paul prays that Israel may attain by coming to believe in Christ through the word of faith that is so near to all, to each and every individual.

10:11 Relying again on the scriptural quote of Isa 28:16, Paul continues the appeal for Israelites to believe by emphasizing the universal availability of faith and hope in Christ: "*Everyone* who believes in him will not be put to shame (by God)."

b. The same Lord will bestow salvation upon all who call upon him in faith.

10:12 This faith and hope is offered to "all." For when it comes to faith in Christ there is no distinction between Jews and Greeks; the same Lord Jesus is the Lord of "all" (see also 3:29–30), who showers his rich salvific benefits upon "all" who call upon him.

10:13 Paul then selects yet another scriptural promise, this one from Joel 3:5, to climax his appeal for "*everyone*," but especially for unbelieving Israelites, to believe by "calling upon the name of the Lord" and thus possessing the sure hope that they "will be saved" by God.

With his determined solicitation for the welfare of his fellow Israelites, Paul has enlightened his readership about the firm hope for God's future and final "salvation" that comes from the faith that is universally near and easily available to all. With the solid support of the scriptural word of God, Paul has thus alerted his audience into absorbing the undeniable fact that the hope for salvation (10:1, 9, 10, 13) remains an open possibility for Israel, if they will only believe.

Through a brisk rhetorical interrogation Paul asserts that all the ingredients necessary for coming to faith are readily at hand for everyone:

5. *Romans 10:14–18:*

14 How then are persons to call upon him in whom they have not believed? How are they to believe in him of whom they have never heard? How are they to hear without a preacher? 15 And how are persons to preach unless they are sent? As it is written, "How timely are the feet of those who have brought good news of good things!" (Isa 52:7). 16 But not all have obeyed the gospel. For Isaiah says, "Lord, who has believed in hearing us?" (Isa 53:1). 17 So faith comes from hearing and hearing comes through the word of Christ. 18 But I ask, have they not heard? Indeed they have: "To all the earth their voice has gone out, and to the ends of the world their words" (Ps 19:4).

a. *The preachers of the word of faith have been sent for all to hear.*

10:14–15 Paul underscores faith's radical nearness and universal availability as he elaborates upon the fact that the "word of faith" has been preached (see 10:8) to everyone throughout the world. Through the device of a concise series of rhetorically protesting questions, Paul lists the necessary ingredients for the chain-like process involved in coming to faith: if "all" are to "call upon" the name of the Lord (10:13), they must first "believe"; if they are to "believe," they must first "hear"; if they are to "hear," there must first be a "preacher"; but before people can "preach" they must first be "sent" to preach by God.

10:15 Paul answers these rhetorical protests by indicating that the preachers have indeed been sent and the gospel is now being heralded in accord with the prophetic exclamation of "how timely[11] are the feet of those (Christian preachers) who have brought good news (the gospel) of good things (God's end-time salvation)!" (Isa 52:7).

b. *All who have not yet believed have heard the word of faith.*

10:16 But despite the fact that Christian preachers have been sent by God, Paul sadly reports that not "all" have "obeyed" by believing in the gospel. So now the lamentful utterance of the prophet Isaiah can be voiced by the present preachers of the gospel, expressing their dismay that although the majority have heard, they have not believed: "Lord, who has believed in hearing us?" (Isa 53:1).

10:17 And so Paul reaffirms that "faith" stems from the act of "hearing," and "hearing" ensues from the "word of Christ," that is, the preached "word" of the gospel in which Christ himself speaks and acts.

10:18 But through diatribal objection Paul insistently contends that those who do not yet believe do in fact already possess this necessary prerequisite for believing—they all "have heard" the "word of Christ." For the announcement of the Psalmist now applies to those who are preaching the gospel and thus indicates the universal extent and availability of the word of Christ: The "voice" of Christian preachers "has gone out *to all the earth*" and "their words *to the ends of the world*" (Ps 19:4).

Through his exquisite selection of scriptural quotes Paul has masterfully convinced his implied readers that the necessary prerequisites for believing—the preaching and hearing by all of the word of Christ—have indeed been fulfilled and are even now present, so that all those, especially Israelites, who have not yet believed in the gospel still have every opportunity to do so and thus to call upon the name of the Lord in order to enjoy the secure hope that they *"will be saved"* (10:13).

Paul continues his diatribal inquiry, centering more explicitly upon the case of unbelieving Israel:

6. Romans 10:19–21:

19 But I ask, did Israel not know? First Moses says, "I will make you jealous of a non-nation; of a non-understanding nation I will make you angry" (Deut 32:21). 20 Then Isaiah dares to say, "I have been found by those not seeking me; I have shown myself to those not asking for me" (Isa 65:1). 21 But before Israel he says, "All the day long I stretch out my hands to a disobedient and contrary people" (Isa 65:2).

a. It is God's plan to make Israel jealous of the Gentiles who precede them in faith.

10:19 Alluding again to the ironical paradox of Gentiles coming to faith in the Messiah of Israel before Israel herself (see 9:30–31), Paul insistently maintains that Israel was already aware that in God's plan for salvation Gentiles would come to faith ahead of them. God already promised Israel through Moses that he would make "you," Israel, "jealous" and "angry" of the "non-nation," "non-understanding" Gentiles (Deut 32:21).

In other words, according to God's scripturally recorded plan, he would cause his chosen people of Israel to become "jealous" and "angry" of the fact that the unchosen, unenlightened Gentiles who do not even comprise a united people or nation would precede Israel in believing.

Here Paul is beginning to allure his listeners into comprehending the intriguing interrelationship in God's plan between the belief of Gentiles and the unbelief of Israel. It is in fulfilling this promise of God by becoming "jealous" of the faith of the "non-understanding," "non-nation" Gentiles that Israel can eventually arrive at faith (see 11:11, 14).

10:20 And there is now a superb reason to enkindle the burning "jealousy" and "anger" of Israel toward the Gentiles. The words of God himself that Isaiah boldly dared to utter have now been fulfilled in the Gentiles' coming to faith prior to Israel: God has allowed himself to be "found" by the Gentiles who did not even "seek" him, and he has "shown" himself to those Gentiles who never even "asked" for him (Isa 65:1).

b. *God is patiently waiting for stubborn Israel to believe.*

10:21 Paul then adroitly employs the next verse from the book of the prophet Isaiah to depict the pathetic contrast between the believing Gentiles and stubbornly unbelieving Israel. It also functions, however, as an earnest plea from God himself for Israel to believe in the gospel: "All the day long," constantly and continually, God extends his open hands toward a "disobedient and contrary people" of Israel (Isa 65:2), patiently waiting for them to seek and find him through faith in Christ.

At this point Paul has intently persuaded his implied readership that the people of Israel have had and still have every opportunity to believe and thus gain the sure hope for God's salvation: there is the appeal that everyone who believes in the "stumbling stone" of Christ "will not be put to shame" (Isa 28:16 in 9:33 and 10:11); although it is defective, Israel nevertheless shows a "zeal for God" (10:2); God has brought Christ and faith in him very near (10:6–8); faith in Christ is available to all (10:9–13); the prerequisites of preaching and hearing the word of Christ have been met for all, including Israel (10:14–18); Israel can now come to faith through "jealousy" of the Gentiles who have believed ahead of them (10:19–20); and God continuously extends an offer for Israel to come to faith (10:21).

The hope for salvation that results from faith is still available to a disobedient Israel, but unfortunately Israel as a whole has, as a pain-fully deplorable fact, not yet believed. And so the question that Paul provokes in the hearts of his readers is: Will this unbelief remain per-manent and become definitive, or will Israel eventually arrive at faith?

D. Rom 11:1–24: The Present Unbelief of Israel Is Interrelated to the Faith of Christians.

Paul returns to the consideration of the perplexing problem of Israel's unbelief primarily from the vantage point of God and his sal-vific plan.

1. Romans 11:1–6:

1 I ask then, has God rejected his people? By no means! For I my-self am an Israelite, a descendant of Abraham, from the tribe of Ben-jamin. 2 God has not rejected his people whom he chose beforehand. Do you not know what the scripture says in (the passage about) Elijah, how he pleads with God against Israel? 3 "Lord, they have killed your prophets, they have destroyed your altars, and I alone am left, and they seek my life" (1 Kgs 19:10, 14). 4 But what is God's reply to him? "I have kept for myself seven thousand men, who have not bowed the knee to Baal" (1 Kgs 19:18). 5 So then also in the present time there is a remnant freely chosen by grace. 6 And if by grace, then no longer from works; otherwise grace would no longer be grace.

a. Paul himself is living proof that God has not definitively rejected his people Israel.

11:1 With rhetorical musing Paul queries his audience into con-sidering whether Israel's continuing, stubborn unbelief means that God has in fact rejected his people. "By no means!" Paul promptly and adamantly protests, for that would imply the absurdity that God has rejected Paul himself, who stands in firm fellowship with Israel as he himself is an Israelite descended from Abraham and belonging to the tribe of Benjamin (see 9:3).

Paul himself, with his authentic Jewish ancestry, embodies the liv-ing proof that God has certainly not rejected or abandoned the very people he long ago chose to be his own. Even if Paul were the only believing, Christian Jew, that would be enough to admit that God has not totally spurned Israel.

11:2–3 And there is scriptural precedent for such an occurrence within God's plan. Paul aligns his own predicament with regard to Israel with that experienced long ago by the prophet Elijah, as he recalls for his listeners the passage (1 Kgs 19:10–18) in which it seems to Elijah that he remains the only Israelite who has not repudiated Yahweh to worship the Canaanite god Baal. If these prophet-killers and followers of a false god succeed in their plot to kill Elijah, then there may be none who remain faithful to the true God, Yahweh.

b. Through God's grace there is even now a freely chosen remnant of Israelites who believe.

11:4 But God responds to Elijah's anguished and lamentful alarm by reassuring him that he has preserved for himself a remnant of seven thousand faithful adherents "who have not bowed the knee to Baal" (1 Kgs 19:18).

11:5 Likewise, at the present time, when Israel as a whole does not believe, Paul pointedly reminds his audience that God has gathered a "remnant" composed of Jewish believers in Christ, "freely chosen by grace." As in the time of Elijah, so now, a hope still lingers for Israel represented by a remnant of believers out of Israel.

11:6 But, as Paul relentlessly emphasizes, it is a hope derived from God's freely given "grace," not on the achievement of the "works" of the Law. For if one could arrive at faith and the hope that accompanies it by meritoriously performing the works of the Law rather than by humbly receiving God's grace, then that "grace" would no longer be what it is, namely, the *freely given,* as opposed to "earned," *gift* of God.

And so Paul's readership must not think that God has completely scorned his own people. Paul and the other Jewish Christians embody evidence to the contrary. Rather, Paul would have his readers still hold out a hope for Israel at this point, a hope encouraged by this believing "remnant" out of Israel.

Paul continues to illustrate for his listeners how the unbelief of Israel as a whole is encompassed within God's plan:

2. Romans 11:7–10:

7 What then? That which Israel seeks, it did not obtain. The elect did obtain it, but the others were hardened, 8 as it is written, "God gave them a spirit of stupor (Isa 29:10), eyes that should not see and ears that should not hear, to this very day" (Deut 29:3). 9 And David says, "Let their table become a snare and a trap, a stumbling stone and

a retribution for them; 10 let their eyes be darkened so that they do
not see, and bend their backs forever" (Ps 69:23–24).

a. An elect number of Jews have believed but the others have been hardened into unbelief.

11:7 At this point Paul summarily clarifies God's salvific plan:
The "righteousness" with God that Israel as a people continually seeks
(see 9:31), they have in fact not attained. The "elect," namely Christian
Jews, did acquire it, but the "others," the non-Christian Jews, "were
hardened" into inert stubbornness by God.

b. The recalcitrant unbelief of most Israelites fulfills God's plan.

11:8 Yet this falls precisely within the parameters of God's plan,
since it fulfills the scriptural prediction that God himself would daze
Israel with a dark and somber "spirit of stupor" (Isa 29:10), blinding
their eyes from seeing with faith, and blocking their ears from hearing
the word of Christ (see 10:14–18), down "to this very day" (Deut 29:3).

11:9–10 And now, the havoc that David once wished God would
wreak upon his dreaded enemies (Ps 69:23–24), he has now inflicted
upon Israel: They repeatedly "stumble" (see 9:32–33) into a trap and
snare of their own making; their eyes have become so unenlightened
that they cannot see the way to faith; indeed, God has forever weighted
down their backs with the burden of unbelief.

Although there are some Jews who have seen the light, heard the
word and believed, Paul has painted a picture that appears very grim
and gloomy indeed for the "others," those Israelites who refuse to believe in Christ. And so Paul has depressed his auditors into wondering
whether there can possibly be any hope at all in God's design for these
still recalcitrant Israelites.

3. Romans 11:11–15:

11 I ask then, have they stumbled so as to fall? By no means! But
by their trespass salvation comes to the Gentiles so as to make them
(Israel) jealous. 12 If their fall means wealth for the world and their
deficiency means wealth for the Gentiles, how much more will their
full number mean! 13 But I speak now to you Gentiles. Inasmuch then
as I am an apostle to the Gentiles, I magnify my ministry, 14 in the
hope that perhaps, somehow, I might make my flesh (Israel) jealous
and save some of them. 15 For if their rejection means reconciliation,
what will their acceptance mean if not life from the dead?

a. Israel's unbelief has brought salvation to the Gentiles to make Israel jealous.

11:11 Through the diatribal manner of rhetorical inquiry Paul invites his readers to ponder whether it is part of God's plan that the "hardened others" in Israel (11:7) have "stumbled" so as to *finally and definitively* "fall" into the hopelessness of obdurate unbelief. "By no means!" Paul insistently thunders. On the contrary, it is through Israel's "fall" into unbelief that God's "salvation" has come to the Gentiles, for the purpose of inciting Israel to "jealousy" (see 10:19).

Obstinate unbelief is not God's final purpose for Israel. Rather, in God's intricate salvific scheme Israel's failure to believe has been instrumental in alluring the Gentiles to faith and thus to hope for salvation. And the Gentiles' arrival at faith through the repudiating unbelief of Israel likewise plays a part in God's future purpose to finally propel unbelieving Israel to faith by igniting in them a burning "jealousy" of the Gentiles.

God's final intent for his people Israel, then, is not a definitive "fall" into inflexible unbelief, but their eventual swing to faith by becoming resentfully "jealous" of the Gentiles' relation to God. Paul has persuaded his audience that within God's wonderfully complex salvific design there is still hope that stubbornly unbelieving Israel will eventually turn to faith, a hope that is interrelated to the faith and hope of the Gentiles.

b. Israel's coming to faith will mean a much greater goal of hope for all.

11:12 Paul begins to explicate this elaborate interrelation by revealing how immensely important Israel's future attainment of faith is for the hope of Paul's readers and all Christians. If the "full number" of the people of Israel comes to faith, then the future eschatological salvation for which all Christians hope will be that much greater.

As Paul enthusiastically reasons, if Israel's fall into unbelief means the "wealth" of God's salvation for the world and if Israel's deficiency in coming to faith means God's saving "wealth" for the Gentiles, how much more bounteous for all will a full number of believing Israelites be!

The future, final salvation, the lavish "wealth," that will follow upon the full number of Israel arriving at faith means a future goal of hope which will far exceed the wonderful "wealth" that has followed upon the miserable failure of Israel as a whole to believe.

c. Paul hopes to bring Israelites to faith through his apostolate to the Gentiles.

11:13–14 Becoming more personal, Paul turns directly to the Gentiles in his audience and apprises them of his own special, apostolic hope (see 1:1–14) of arousing Israel to faith. As an impassioned and devoted "apostle to the Gentiles" Paul purposefully amplifies his ministry toward them in the hope that perhaps, in some way, he might instigate his fellow Israelites to covetous "jealousy" of the faith of the Gentiles and thereby rescue some of them by compelling them to believe in the gospel.

It is part of Paul's hope as an apostle, then, that his ministry of evangelizing Gentiles to obedient faith (see 1:5) will be incorporated into God's universal salvific plan of eventually leading Israel as a whole to faith. Paul informs his Gentile readers that his apostolic ministry to them has an interrelation and an ulterior motive with regard to Israel's future procurement of faith.

11:15 There is an interrelation because not only will the coming to faith of Gentiles profit unbelieving Israel by exciting them to envy, but, conversely, Israel's future attainment of faith will benefit Gentiles by bringing about an even greater future goal of hope for all. For if Israel's "rejection" by God, in their not yet believing in his gospel, means "reconciliation" with God for the rest of the world, their "acceptance" by God, in their eventual arrival at faith, will surely mean nothing less than the esteemed and hoped for "life from the dead"!

Through the rhetorical device of speaking directly to the Gentiles, Paul has forcefully impressed upon his readership how enormously significant Israel's future coming to faith remains for the hope of Paul, Gentiles and all Christians. Israel's future believing in the gospel about Christ will mean a tremendously greater future goal of hope not only for the Gentiles but for the whole world—God's future, final and eternal "life from the dead"!

4. Romans 11:16–21:

16 If the first-fruit is holy, so is the mass; and if the root is holy, so are the branches. 17 But if some of the branches have been broken off, and you, a wild olive shoot, have been grafted in among them and have become a sharer in the rich root of the olive tree, 18 do not boast against the branches. For if you boast against them, remember that you do not support the root but the root supports you. 19 You will say then, "Branches were broken off in order that I might be grafted

in." 20 That is true. Because of their unbelief they were broken off, and because of your faith you remain. Do not think proud thoughts, but stand in awe. 21 For if God did not spare the natural branches, then he will certainly not spare you!

a. There is hope for the future coming to faith of Israel based on her holy origins.

11:16 Having broadened the goal of the hope of all Christians by adding to it the hope for Israel's future faith, Paul reminds his Gentile readers that their Christian hope ultimately rests upon the sacred origins of the people of Israel.

The hope for Israel's future attainment of faith is anchored in Israel's "holy first-fruits" and "holy root": If the initial dough that was offered in worship to God as "first-fruit" of the harvest is consecrated and revered as "holy" (see Num 15:17–21), then so is the rest of the lump or mass of dough; similarly, if the root of God's special olive tree that figuratively characterizes the people of Israel is considered "holy," then so are the branches of the tree, namely, individual Israelites.[12]

There is yet hope that God will coax the holy "branches," individual Israelites, to faith because of their "holy root," the honored patriarchs of Israel (see 11:28).

b. Gentile Christians should not scorn unbelieving Israelites whose holy origins support Gentile faith.

11:17–18 Employing a more direct, personal and individualized (second person singular) address while further developing his artful, horticultural imagery, Paul warns Gentile Christians not to "boast against" the branches of the olive tree which is Israel, just because some of the branches, unbelieving Israelites, have been "broken off" by God through their unbelief. For "you," the Gentile who represents a wild olive shoot, have been grafted in among the believing Israelites and have become a fortunate sharer in the rich root (the legacy of the patriarchs) of the olive tree.

And if the Christian Gentile should arrogantly imagine himself superior to unbelieving Israelites and thus "boast against" the "branches," Paul alertly cautions and reminds him that "*you*," the engrafted branch, certainly do not support the root of the olive tree, but, on the contrary, the firm and solid root sustains you.

It would be a terribly insolent presumption for Christian Gentiles to boast or vaunt themselves over the Israelites, for then they would be ignorantly failing to realize that their hope as Christians has its true and firm foundation in the very same "holy" and "rich root" which they share with the Israelite "branches." In other words, the Christian hope of which Gentiles can legitimately "boast" (see 5:2–11) is soundly and unmistakably "rooted" in Israel's holy origins (the patriarchs) so that there is absolutely no room for Gentile Christians to harbor a supercilious disdain for Israelites.

c. Paul warns Gentile Christians to humbly appreciate and persevere in their faith.

11:19 Continuing his rhetorical dialogue with an imaginary, individual Gentile, Paul admits the truth of the Gentile's claim that Israelite "branches" were broken off from the root of the tree in order that "I," the Gentile, might be grafted in.

11:20 But he recalls for the Gentile that his having been grafted into the holy root of Israel depends solely and totally on his God-given faith. It is only because of their unfortunate unbelief that Israelites have been broken off from the root, but, on the other hand, it is only because of their faith that Gentiles remain grafted into the root of the tree. Therefore, the Gentile Christian should not swell up with haughtiness by thinking "proud" thoughts but should rather stand in fearfully reverent awe and humility before God.

11:21 For, as Paul forewarns his Gentile partner, if God did not spare the natural branches who did not believe, then he will obviously not spare "you," the Gentile, if "you" are not fortunate enough to persevere in believing. While averting his audience from a scornful spurning of unbelieving Israelites, Paul has awakened in them a reverent appreciation and humble gratitude to God for their own Christian faith.

Still speaking to the individual Gentile Christian, Paul deftly illustrates for his listeners how wholly and radically dependent Christian faith is upon God:

5. Romans 11:22–24:

22 Consider then the kindness and severity of God: severity toward those who have fallen, but the kindness of God toward you, provided that you remain in his kindness, otherwise you also will be cut off! 23 But even those others, if they do not remain in unbelief, will be grafted in, for God has the power to graft them in again. 24 For if you have been cut off from what is by nature a wild olive tree and contrary to nature have been grafted into a cultivated olive tree, how much more will these natural branches be grafted back into their own olive tree!

a. Gentiles have come to faith by the kindness of God who also has the power to bring Israel to faith.

11:22 Through dialogue with his Gentile partner Paul prods his audience to ponder the "kindness" and "severity" of God—his harsh severity is painfully evident upon those Israelites who can be considered to have "fallen" because he has not yet brought them to faith, and his gracious "kindness" is clearly apparent as it has descended upon "*you*," the Gentile, whom he has benevolently guided to faith. But, as Paul sternly admonishes and alarms the Gentile Christian, "you" must remain in his kindness by persevering in faith; otherwise "you" also will be cleanly severed from the root.

11:23 And conversely, if God mercifully leads individual Israelites out of the dismal darkness of unbelief and into the splendid light of faith, then we may all have the hope that they "will be grafted" back into the holy root. And this fresh hope for Israelites that Paul now sparks in his listeners flows from the majestic "power" of God to induce them to faith, for as Paul confesses and as his readers must admit, the omnipotent God certainly "has the power to graft them in again."

b. The hope is sure that God can easily bring Israelites to faith by grafting them back into their own holy root.

11:24 With consummate skill Paul masterfully molds his cleverly enlightening and supremely appropriate imagery of the olive tree into a rousing climax. He strengthens the hope for Israelites by interrelating it to the manifestation of God's kindly "power" toward the Gentiles. If God lustrously exhibited his salvific "power" in cutting "you," the Gentile, from what is by nature a wild olive tree, and graciously grafting "you" against nature into the cultivated olive tree of Israel, then how much more certainly will God display his salvific "power" by grafting the natural branches, individual Israelites, back into *their own olive tree!*

The hope that Israelites "*will be grafted*" back into what is *their own* olive tree by finally coming to faith depends upon and is stimulated by the salvific "power" of God, a power which Paul has reminded his readers that they themselves have wonderfully experienced and beheld in God's "grafting" in of the Gentiles by guiding them to faith.

And so Paul has fascinatingly lured and enticed his readership to the daringly bold but certain hope that the same almighty God who mercifully bestowed faith on the uncultivated, "wild olive tree" of the Gentiles can and will surely grant faith to the holy, richly rooted (11:17–18) and "cultivated olive tree" of Israelites.

E. Rom 11:25–36: Paul Proclaims the Hope That All Israel Will Be Saved So That God Might Have Mercy on Us All.

Having aroused his readers to the hope that God can and will bring the "branches" of the olive tree, individual unbelieving Israelites, to faith, Paul now goes one step further and arrives at a full, climactic and universal hope for all Israel as a people.

1. Romans 11:25–27:

25 I want you indeed to understand, brothers, this mystery, lest you become wise in your own estimation, that a hardening has come upon part of Israel until the full number of Gentiles come in, 26 and thus all Israel will be saved! As it is written,

> "Out of Zion will come the Deliverer,
>   he will turn away ungodliness from Jacob;
> 27 and this will be my covenant for them,
>   when I take away their sins" (Isa 59:20–21; 27:9).

a. The mystery of God's plan provides the sure hope that all Israel will be saved!

11:25–26 With the rhetorically emphatic formula, "I want you indeed to understand,"[13] Paul stresses the great importance of "this mystery" of God's hidden salvific plan that Paul is about to reveal to his fellow Christian readers. This secret and intricate "mystery" that Paul unravels and communicates to his listeners explains the way that God will save the whole people of Israel: The "hardening" of unbelief that God has allowed to prevail over part of Israel is only temporary; it will remain only until it has completed its respective role within God's intended scheme of embracing the full number (as determined by God) of Gentiles into the community of end-time salvation (see 11:11, 17), and "thus," *in this way*, "all Israel will be saved!"

In other words, if the present unbelief of "part" of Israel is only temporary and, moreover, if it serves God's salvific purpose of leading the "full number" of Gentiles to faith, then this mysterious design of God motivates Paul to share with his fellow Christians his sure hope that "thus" *all* Israel will be saved!

This enlarged hope that "*all*" Israel as a people "will be *saved*" represents the stimulating high point of the gradually and dramatically increasing hope for the *salvation* of the people of Israel that Paul has been adroitly and ingeniously unfolding throughout Romans 9—11, so that Israel as a whole will no longer be an unbelieving, "disobedient and contrary people" (10:21):

FAITH AND THE HOPE FOR ISRAEL'S SALVATION

9:27:   If the number of the sons of Israel be as the sand of the sea, a remnant *will be saved!*

10:1:   Brothers, my heart's desire and prayer to God for them is for their *salvation.*

10:9:   If you confess with your mouth that Jesus is Lord and believe in your heart that God raised him from the dead, you *will be saved!*

10:10:   For with the heart a person believes for righteousness, and with the mouth a person confesses for *salvation.*

10:13:   For everyone who calls upon the name of the Lord *will be saved!*

11:13–14: I magnify my ministry, in the hope that perhaps, somehow, I might make my flesh (Israel) jealous and *save* some of them.

11:26:   And thus all Israel WILL BE SAVED!

The hope that all Israel will be saved carries important consequences for the rest of Christian hope. Paul informs his Christian readers of "this mystery" lest they become "wise in their own estimation."

He already warned Gentile Christians against "boasting over" Israel (11:18), a misguided and arrogant presumption because it neglects to recognize that Christian hope for future "salvation" (11:11) and "life from the dead" (11:15) is ultimately anchored in Israel's "holy root," the patriarchal promises of old. Paul also admonished them against "thinking proud thoughts" based on their present situation of faith (11:20); such a pride rising from one's own standing in faith is tantamount to a haughty overconfidence because it fails to realize that "faith" is not ultimately one's own doing but a gracious gift from God.

And now Paul carefully cautions his fellow Christians against a hope which relies upon their own human wisdom, as he introduces them to God's wisdom (see 11:33) with its expansive hope that *all* Israel will be saved. A hope which depends upon our own human way of thinking about Israel's future due to Israel's present unbelief would needlessly constrain and limit the future goal of our Christian hope, but "this mystery" of God's intricate and intriguing salvific scheme broadens the future goal of our hope to include and embrace the salvation of *all* Israel.

b. *All Israel will be saved by coming to believe in their own Messiah.*

11:26–27 Again calling upon the powerful and never failing word of God in scripture, Paul boosts the certainty of the hope that he is arousing in his audience for all Israel to be saved. With a combined prophetic promise for future salvation from Isa 59:20–21 and 27:9, whose fulfillment is assured because it is the unfailing word of God (see 9:6), Paul confirms the hope for the future salvation of all Israel in accord with "this mystery" of God's salvific design.

Through this scriptural promise Paul reminds his listeners that it is "out of Zion," the revered and holy foundation of Israel, that the "Deliverer" of God's people will come and remove the "ungodliness" of unbelief from "Jacob," that is, Israel as personified in the blessed patriarch Jacob.

The fact that the Christ has already emerged from Israel (see 1:3; 9:5) as the Deliverer of God's people strengthens the hope of this promise for Paul's Christian readers, who have already experienced these promised salvific benefits. They are confidently assured that God will turn away the "ungodliness" of Israel and manifest his covenant fidelity on behalf of Israel by forgiving their sins. This prophetic scriptural promise thus implies that presently unbelieving Israel will be saved, like Christians, by finally believing in God's justification of their "ungodliness" through Christ's death and in God's forgiveness of their sins (see 4:5–8; 3:23–26; 5:6–8).

By further delineating the interrelated roles of Israel and the Gentiles within God's mysterious plan for universal salvation, Paul further bolsters the hope of his audience for all Israel to be saved:

2. *Romans 11:28–32:*

28 With regard to the gospel they are enemies for your sake; but with regard to election they are beloved because of the patriarchs. 29 For the gifts and the call of God are irrevocable. 30 Just as you were once disobedient to God, but now have received mercy because of their disobedience, 31 so also they have now been disobedient for the benefit of the mercy shown to you, in order that they may now

receive mercy. 32 For God has imprisoned all in disobedience, in order that he may have mercy on all!

a. The hope for all Israel is based upon her unique role in God's plan and upon God's election and call of Israel's patriarchs.

11:28 As he nears the conclusion of his concerted argumentation concerning the problem of unbelieving Israel, Paul discloses a final, climactic and summarizing insight into the marvelous "mystery" of God's salvific purpose, a privileged insight aimed at inducing his readership to join him in the hope for God's universal salvation. The unique role that Israel plays within God's plan of salvation makes the hope that all Israel will be saved all the more certain for Paul's readers.

That Israelites, as unbelievers, are "enemies" of God as regards the spreading of the gospel serves a positive function within God's salvific design, since it is "for *your* sake," that is, for *your* belief in the gospel which brings you salvation. Paul thus compels "you," his Christian auditors, to realize and appreciate the fact that, from the viewpoint of God's salvific purpose, Israel's unbelief has been enormously beneficial for spreading belief in the gospel to Christians, especially Gentile Christians.

Furthermore, as regards God's previous "election" the Israelites are still "beloved" by God because they remain physical descendants of the great patriarchs.

11:29 And since the "gifts" (see 9:4–5) and the "call" of election that God has already graciously bestowed upon Israel through their forefathers, the patriarchs (see 9:6–13), are permanent and thus "irrevocable," they still serve as a solid foundation of hope for Israel.

b. The mercy that God has already granted Gentiles stimulates the hope for the mercy of God upon Israel and all other peoples.

11:30–31 The hope that *all* Israel will be saved within God's overall salvific scheme acquires even greater assurance for Paul's audience as he demonstrates how it is stimulated by the *"mercy"* that God has already granted to "you," Paul's Christian readers, precisely because of Israel's unbelief. And that God will ultimately display his "mercy" to all Israel just as he has already manifested mercy to "you" Christians illustrates why Christians should not cling to a narrow and limited hope which relies on their own human wisdom, but should expand and extend the future goal of their hope to embrace God's mercy and salvation for *all*—both the Gentiles and Israel.

For, according to the insight that Paul reveals into God's secret plan, just as "you" Christians once were "disobedient" to God by not believing, but now have received God's mercy because of Israel's "disobedience" of unbelief, so they have now been "disobedient" for the benefit of the mercy shown to you, in order that they may now receive God's mercy!

Because the respective salvation-historical roles of the Gentiles and of Israel have been so inextricably interwoven by God, the hope is sure that just as God's mercy has already begun to overcome the disobedient unbelief of the Gentiles, as Paul's audience can easily verify by looking at themselves, so "*now*" in the time open to God's eschatological future which has already commenced, God's mercy will certainly overcome the disobedient unbelief of Israel.

11:32 Paul then caps off this amplified hope which we Christians may now foster toward "all," as inspired by the mercy God has already graciously conferred upon us: For God has enclosed and "imprisoned" *all* in the disobedience of first not believing, in order that he may then have mercy on *all*, Gentiles and Israel, by leading them to faith and salvation.

And so, Paul has stirred his audience to realize that since it is based on the unbounded, universal mercy of God, authentic Christian hope can and must remain radically open to the future of God—to the future manifestation of his mercy and salvation for all, including *all* Israel.

MERCY IN GOD'S PLAN FOR UNIVERSAL SALVATION

9:15:   For he says to Moses, "I will have *mercy* on whom I have *mercy* . . .

9:16:   So then (the purpose of God depends) not upon anyone's willing nor upon anyone's striving, but upon God's showing of *mercy*.

9:18:   So then he has *mercy* on whomever he wills . . .

9:23:   . . . in order to make known the wealth of his glory upon vessels of *mercy* . . .

11:30:   Just as you were once disobedient to God, but now have received *mercy* because of their disobedience,

11:31:   so also they have now been disobedient for the benefit of the *mercy* shown to you, in order that they may now receive *mercy*.

11:32:   For God has imprisoned all in disobedience, so that HE MAY HAVE MERCY ON ALL!

Bringing his exciting and encouraging appeal that his readers have hope for God's salvation of all of Israel to a fitting climax, Paul exuberantly and eloquently praises God as he stands in awe of the tremendous magnificence of God's wonderfully grand plan for universal salvation:

3. Romans 11:33–36:

33 Oh the depth of the riches and wisdom and knowledge of God! How unsearchable his decisions and inscrutable his ways! 34 For,

> "Who has known the mind of the Lord,
>   or who has been his adviser? (Isa 40:13).
> 35 Or who has given to him beforehand,
>   so that he might be repaid?" (Job 35:7; 41:11).

36 For from him and through him and to him are all things! To him be glory forever! Amen!

a. Paul invites Christians to stand in awe of God's marvelous scheme for universal salvation.

11:33 In view of the humanly incomprehensible "mystery" (11:25) of God's plan which arouses the hope that *all* Israel will be saved and that God will have mercy on *all,* Paul invites his audience to join him in his effusive outburst of humble awe in view of the overwhelming and unfathomable depth of the "riches" and "wisdom" and "knowledge" of God.

The riches (see 9:23; 11:12), wisdom and knowledge of God are evident in the unique and unusual way in which he has intertwined the unbelief of Israel with the belief of Christians in his complex design for universal salvation. As Paul has just illustrated throughout Romans 9–11, the decisions God makes and the ways in which he works out his salvific scheme are humanly "unsearchable" and totally "inscrutable."

Through this admiration for the details of God's wonderful plan for salvation, which transcend the capabilities of the human mind, Paul induces his readers to realize that in their Christian hope for future salvation they cannot rely on merely human wisdom but must remain completely open and ready for God's incomprehensible future.

b. No human being can fully comprehend the wonderful wisdom of God's plan for the salvation of all.

11:34–35 Paul again selects a scriptural word of God as testimony to prove to his listeners that there is indeed no human being who can fully fathom the mind of God, no one who can ever serve as his counselor or adviser (Isa 40:13), and no one who can place God in his debt (Job 35:7; 41:11).

He thus persuades his auditors to acknowledge that there is no human being who can calculate or control, comprehend or fully grasp, the unfathomable riches, wisdom and knowledge of God. In view of the unlimited greatness of God and his magnificent plan for universal salvation, Christians must keep themselves radically ready and open for God's incalculable and uncontrollable future. As Paul has convincingly demonstrated in Romans 9—11, God's power and will to save far exceeds what human beings can think or imagine.

c. Paul summons Christians to praise the God of unlimited hope.

11:36 With an animated and inspiring closing doxology which acknowledges that "all things" not only came "from" and "through" God but have their future, final goal "in" God, Paul puts the final touch on his impressive illustration that in their hope Christians must look to the humanly unfathomable ways of God for the future salvation of all. It is the creating and saving God who holds ultimate power and control over all things, so that the incalculably great God stands as the origin, the agent and the future goal of Christian hope for the merciful salvation of all of humanity. Paul's readers can only echo his words of grateful praise—"To him be glory forever! Amen!"

F. Summary

After drawing his audience into his sincere and serious concern for his fellow Israelites who do not yet believe in their own Messiah, Paul reassured his listeners that despite this deplorable unbelief of Israel God's word has not failed (9:6). As the word of God has always operated through the principle of God's free election and mercy, it continues to be a strong and valid foundation for the hope of Christians (9:22–26), and the enduring word and salvific purpose of God still supports a hope for unbelieving Israel as well (9:27–29).

Despite every opportunity provided by God Israel as a people has stubbornly refused to believe in the gospel (9:30—10:21). But Paul alerted his auditors to the fact that faith is still available to Israel. All the ingredients they need to turn and submit themselves in faith to the gospel about Christ are patiently staring them in the face. In order to enjoy the same hope for God's promised salvation as Paul's Christian readers, all they have to do is believe (11:19–21).

Since arriving at and remaining in faith depends ultimately upon God's free gift, Paul advised his audience that their attitude of Christian hope must include a reverent and humble respect of God. God has not abandoned his chosen people, Israel. Some of them, including Paul himself, do believe (11:1–10). The failure of most of Israel to believe, however, serves God's salvific design by allowing the Gentiles to come to faith and thus make Israel so jealous that they will eventually believe as well (11:11–24). Paul thus averted his Christian readers from "boasting over" Israel (11:18), becoming arrogantly proud of their own status in faith (11:20), and being wise in their own estimation about the future of God (11:25).

Paul urged his readership to remain ready and open to the future of the sovereign God who freely calls (9:12) and shows his mercy (9:16, 23–26). In accord with the secret mystery of God's grand plan of salvation, Paul, with considerable delight, stirred his listeners to expand their Christian hope to embrace the daringly bold but sure hope that "all Israel will be saved!" (11:25–27). He excited his audience with the optimistic thought that Israel's future coming to faith by becoming jealous of the Gentiles will mean an even greater future goal for Christian hope (11:11–15). Paul's Christian readers may now enjoy the electrifying hope that God will dispense and disseminate his great mercy to "all" (11:28–32), so that the hope of Christians can and must remain radically open to the awesomely incalculable, uncontrollable and limitless future salvation of all of God's creation (11:33–36).

In reaching the climactic and conclusive hope that all Israel will be saved, as God will eventually and finally bestow his gracious mercy upon all, Paul has furthered his stated purpose of encouraging and strengthening the hope of his fellow Christians (1:11–12). In so doing he has pushed the future goal of Christian hope beyond the bounds of human understanding; it is the future *of God himself*—a future of unlimited and total salvation which far exceeds human expectation and imagination, for "*all things* are from him and through him and to him; glory be to him forever! Amen!"

NOTES

1. As J. W. Aageson ["Scripture and Structure in the Development of the Argument in Romans 9–11," *CBQ* 48 (1986) 286] insightfully indicates: "The reliability of *God's word* to Israel was at stake; and it was to *God's word*, the Scriptures, that Paul turned to argue that it had not failed."

2. There is a certain precedent for this kind of wish in the intercessory prayer of Moses on behalf of Israel in Exod 32:32.

3. The translation of Paul's spontaneous blessing is notoriously difficult. We have attempted to remain as faithful as possible to the original Greek, which is somewhat ambiguous, perhaps purposely so, as to whether the praise is directed to Christ, God or both. See B. M. Metzger, *A Textual Commentary on the Greek New Testament* (London/New York: United Bible Societies, 1971) 520–523.

4. "Has not failed" (*ouk ekpeptoken*) is in the perfect tense meaning "has not failed (in the past) and still is not failing (in the present)."

5. "The purpose of God" in Rom 9:11 should be understood as the subject of Rom 9:16. See M. Zerwick and M. Grosvenor, *A Grammatical Analysis of the Greek New Testament* (2 vols.; Rome: Biblical Institute, 1974, 1979) 480.

6. "Israel" in 9:27 refers to unbelieving Israelites. Paul employs the term "Jews" in 9:24 to refer to those Israelites who have believed. That these believing "Jews" are part of a "remnant" of Israel will be expressed later in Romans 11, but in 9:27–29 Paul is concerned with the future hope for a remnant from those Israelites who presently do not believe.

7. Many translate the quotation in 9:27 as a concessive clause and add an "only" in the apodosis: "Although the number of the sons of Israel be as the sand of the sea, only a remnant will be saved." They thus interpret this to be a "limiting" judgment on Israel. But we follow S. Lyonnet (*Quaestiones in Epistulam ad Romanos. Series Altera. Rom 9–11* [3d ed.; Rome: Biblical Institute, 1975] 74–80) in considering the quote in 9:27 to be an "eventual" conditional clause so that if any word is to be added to the apodosis, it would be "surely" and/or "at least" rather than "only," thus: "If the number of the sons of Israel be as the sand of the sea, surely at least a remnant will be saved!"

8. "Not being put to shame" expresses hope in Romans; in 1:16 Paul's "not being ashamed" expresses his confident hope in the gospel and in 5:5 Christian "hope does not shame," that is, it is guaranteed by God.

9. The meaning of "Christ is the end of the Law" in Rom 10:4 is hotly debated by Pauline scholars. The problem centers on whether "end" (*telos*) signifies "end" in the sense of "termination" or "end" in the sense of "goal," "completion" or "fulfillment" of the Law, or perhaps carries both connotations. Because of the immediate context, which accentuates the replacement of righteousness by doing the Law with righteousness by faith in Christ, we follow those who opt for "end" in the sense of the "termination" of the Law; see O. Michel, *Der Brief an die Römer* (MeyerK 4; 14th ed.; Göttingen: Vandenhoeck & Ruprecht, 1978) 326–327; H. Schlier, *Der Römerbrief* (HTKNT 6; Freiburg/Basel/Wien: Herder, 1977) 311; E. Käsemann, *Commentary on Romans* (Grand Rapids: Eerdmans, 1980) 282–283. For a fuller discussion of the problem, see R. Badenas, *Christ The End of the Law: Romans 10.4 in Pauline Perspective* (JSNTSup 10; Sheffield: JSOT, 1985).

10. Note how the use of the second person singular pronouns emphasizes the personal and individual character of the address.

11. We prefer to translate *horaioi* as "timely" rather than the usual "beautiful," because of the emphasis on the eschatological "timeliness" of the arrival of the gospel; see BAGD, 896.

12. The figure of the olive tree to depict Israel as God's special people has biblical basis in Jer 11:16–17: "The Lord once called you (Israel), 'A green olive tree, fair with beautiful fruit'; but . . . its branches will be consumed. The Lord of hosts, who planted you . . ." The image may have been suggested by the olive trees in the confines of the Temple; see Ps 52:8.

13. Note the other occurrences of this formula in Rom 1:13; 1 Cor 10:1; 12:1; 2 Cor 1:8; 1 Thes 4:13.

Chapter VII

Romans 12:1–15:13

A. Rom 12:1–13:14: Live Now in Accord with Your Hope for the Future.

With great enthusiasm and exuberance Paul finely executed his eager intention to encourage and spiritually strengthen his implied readership (1:11–12) by spurring them on to the absolutely assured and certain hope for God's future salvation that they may enjoy as a consequence of their justification by faith in the gospel about Jesus Christ (Romans 1–8). Continuing to encourage his audience, he stirringly reaffirmed and expanded this superb hope to embrace God's future salvation of *all*, including presently unbelieving Israel (Romans 9–11).

Now, in Romans 12:1–15:13, Paul exhorts, encourages and directs his listeners to the way of communal Christian living and everyday practical conduct that naturally flows from and comprises an integral component of the gospel of hope that he has been proclaiming to them. Through this more formally exhortatory and parenetic segment of his Epistle Paul extends and applies the reality of God's justification by faith and consequent hope to the concrete realm of the everyday lives of his Christian readers.

Paul energetically initiates his parenesis with a general and fundamental exhortation that establishes the context and sets the tone for his subsequent exhortations:

1. Romans 12:1–2:

1 I exhort you then, brothers, by the mercies of God to offer your persons as a living sacrifice, holy and pleasing to God, your spiritual worship! 2 Do not conform yourself to this present age, but be continually transformed by the renewal of your mind, so that you may determine what is the will of God, what is good and pleasing and perfect!

a. In response to his mercies Christians are to spiritually and mentally dedicate their lives to God.

12:1 As a consequence of all the many "mercies of God" that he has previously illustrated and proclaimed throughout Romans 1–11, Paul fraternally exhorts his fellow Christian readers to dedicate themselves anew to God. That God has now graciously justified sinners through the "mercy" of his forgiveness (1:16–17; 3:21–4:25), has displayed the "mercy" of his love for us as sinners (5:1–11; 8:31–39), and that God "will have mercy" on all (11:32), including all Israel (11:26), as he has already bestowed his "mercy" on Christians (9:15, 23–25; 11:30–32) exemplify the "mercies of God" by which Paul stimulates his audience to gratefully offer their lives in service to God.

With a surprising twist on his figurative application of technical cultic terms to the new Christian way of life, Paul indicates the totally self-giving response to God's mercies that is now possible and appropriate from his readers. They are to "offer" their bodies or persons as a *living* "sacrifice." Whereas sacrifices normally involve the destruction or death of something that is to be set apart and consecrated to God, Christians are to dedicate their *living* persons as a "sacrifice" set apart to be "holy" and "pleasing" to God.

In contrast to the external, physical rites normally involved in the cultic service of sacrificing, this "pleasing" or "acceptable" sacrificial worship of Christians is to be a worship of the mind and spirit. It is a spiritual, mental consecration of their lives, which can now be "pleasing" to God, whereas those who are "in the flesh" can never "please" God (see 8:8).

Paul previously exhorted his Christian readership to consider themselves already "dead" to the destructive power of sin, but "living" to God (6:11). Christians can and must "offer" themselves "to God" as those who have been brought from the hopelessness of being "dead" to the hope of "living" (6:13). And they must now "offer" the members of their bodies as slaves to God's righteousness which leads to their "holiness" by being sanctified by God (6:19). Similarly, Paul now incites his audience to "offer" themselves as a "living" sacrifice, "holy" and pleasing "to God."

b. Christians who have been spiritually and mentally renewed can and must conform themselves to the will of God.

12:2 In correspondence to the apocalyptic-eschatological dualism of the two ages—this present age and the future age to come—Paul urges his Christian readers not to "conform" themselves to or be

guided by "this present age." Christians are to live their lives already
in accord with God's future "age to come" by continually and critically
distancing themselves from "this present age," the hopeless age which
is gripped and entrapped by the powers of sin and death.

Christians can accomplish this by allowing themselves to be continually "transformed" by the "renewal of their mind," their renewed
way of thinking. Paul earlier explained how we baptized Christians can
already live the future "life" for which we hope by "walking," that is,
conducting ourselves or living, in *"newness* of life" (6:4). We have been
freed from our old captivity to hopelessness under the Law, so that we
can now live out our future hope by serving God in the *"newness* of the
Spirit" (7:6).[1]

Similarly, the *"renewal* of the mind" or the renewed way of thinking and perceiving that is a present Christian prerogative must be allowed to continually transform our present lives, so that they conform
not to "this present age" but to our future hope, God's age to come.

As Paul expatiates, this renewed manner of thinking now enables
us Christians to "determine," "decide" or "discern" what is the "will of
God" in our everyday living. In other words, we now can and must do
that which is "good" and "pleasing" and "perfect," that which is completely in accord with God's will or purpose, in our everyday Christian
behavior and conduct.

In our former hopelessness to the indwelling power of sin under
the Law (7:7–25) it was impossible to do what was "good" (7:18–20),
the "good" commandment or will of God (7:12). But we are now empowered by God's fresh renewing of our mind and thoughts to do "the
good," the "will of God," in our everyday living and thereby conform
and mold our Christian lives to the future, final "good" for which we
ardently hope (see 8:28; 10:15).

Paul thus persuades his Christian auditors that by doing "the
good" now they are promoting and maintaining their Christian hope
for God's future salvation.

2. *Romans 12:3–8:*

3 For by the grace given me I beseech each one among you not to
overstrive beyond what is necessary to strive but strive so as to strive
prudently, each in accord with the measure of faith God has appor-
tioned. 4 For just as in one body we have many members, and all the
members do not have the same function, 5 so we, the many, are one
body in Christ, individually members with one another. 6 Having
charisms which differ according to the grace given us, (let us exercise

them properly): if prophecy, (then let it be done) in proportion to our faith; 7 if service, then in accord with serving; if one teaches, then (let him use his charism) by teaching; 8 if one exhorts, then (let him use his charism) by exhorting; let one who contributes do so with generosity; let one who gives aid do so with diligence; let one who shows mercy do so with cheerfulness.

a. Each member of the one body of Christ must use his/her particular gift for the good of the whole community.

12:3 Directly addressing each individual member of the Christian community at Rome, Paul utilizes a crisp play on words (*hyperphronein/phronein/sophronein,* "overstrive/strive/strive prudently") to pointedly enhance his exhortation about the proper functioning of charisms within the Christian community. By the authority of the God-given "grace" of his apostleship (see 1:5) Paul earnestly entreats each and every Christian not to abuse the particular gift or charism God has given him/her for the edification of the community. No Christian should in overeagerness or self-interest exceed the limits of his/her charism by "overstriving" or "overaspiring" in the exercise of the charism beyond what is "necessary," that is, in accord with God's will for the good of the community. Each should be careful to use his/her particular gift prudently and in proportion to the amount of faith God has granted.

12:4–5 Paul then quite appropriately compares the correct and harmonious functioning of the various charisms in the Christian community with the proper functioning and interrelation of the diverse parts of the human body. Just as the human body is composed of a network of many different individual but mutually related members which do not all serve the same purpose, so the many different members of the Christian community form "one body in Christ" and each individual member is interrelated to all the other members of that "body."

b. The Christian community operates as the one body of Christ through the proper exercise of a variety of charisms.

12:6 Since the Christian community as the "one body of Christ" is blessed by God with a rich diversity of gifts or charisms, each member of that "body" who is so gifted must take it upon himself or herself to utilize his/her particular charism in the best possible way for the overall benefit and enrichment of the "body."

For example, if someone possesses the gift of "prophecy," that is, the divinely inspired ability to pronounce and apply the word of God for the welfare and edification of the other members of the Christian community, then that person must take care to perform that particular charism precisely in proportion to the level of faith in the community so that it can be properly and well received. Otherwise, it will not benefit the "one body of Christ."

12:7 Likewise, the charism of "serving" the other members of the Christian community must be fittingly performed in accord with the norms for such "service." And anyone who "teaches" the other members of the one body of Christ must exercise that particular charism in no other way than by "teaching."

12:8 One who has been blessed with the gift of "exhorting" or "comforting" the Christian community should perform that proper function precisely and without any deviation. The person who "contributes" or "distributes" something to the other members of the community must use that charism to its full extent by contributing with liberal generosity. One who gives "assistance" or "aid" to the other members of the body of Christ should execute that particular charism with "diligence." And the one who has the gift to extend "mercy" to the other members of the community should discharge that function with "cheerfulness."

Paul thus pointedly prods his readers to the full and appropriate use of the respective and special charisms God has granted them, so that the joint and mutual responsibility all Christians have for suitably edifying the "one body of Christ" might be realized.

3. Romans 12:9–21:

9 Let your love be genuine; abhor the evil, adhere to the good; 10 be warmly affectionate toward one another in fraternal love; outdo one another in showing respect. 11 Do not wane in zeal, be inflamed with the Spirit, serve the Lord. 12 Rejoice in hope, be steadfast in suffering, remain constant in prayer. 13 Contribute to the needs of the saints, practice hospitality. 14 Bless those who persecute you, bless rather than curse them. 15 Rejoice with those who are joyful, weep with those who are weeping. 16 Have the same regard for one another, do not dwell on proud thoughts but associate with the lowly; never be conceited among yourselves. 17 Do not repay to anyone evil with evil, but plan beforehand for what is agreeable in the eyes of all. 18 If possible on your part, live in peace with all. 19 Beloved, never avenge yourselves, but rather give place to the wrath (of God); for it is written, "Vindication is mine, I will repay" (Deut 32:35), says the Lord. 20 But, "if your enemy is hungry, feed him; if he is thirsty, give

him drink; for by so doing you will heap burning coals upon his head" (Prov 25:21–22). 21 Do not be conquered by the evil, but rather conquer the evil with the good.

a. There should be a warm, affectionate and genuine love operative within the Christian community.

12:9 From the love that should govern the performance of the special charisms given to members of the community (12:3–8), Paul moves to more general exhortations involving Christian communal love. The Pauline notion of "love" (*agape*) here refers to the active care and concern Christians are to show one another. Such love should be sincere, genuine and without pretense.

If such love is to prevail in the community, then Christians must "abhor" or "avoid" whatever is evil for the community and "cling" or "adhere" to that which is good for the community. Thus Christians must distance themselves completely from what is bad and dedicate themselves totally to what is of benefit for the community.

12:10 As Paul continues his urging he further describes the intensely optimistic and upbeat character of the love he envisions to rule over the Christian community. Authentic Christian love should be warmly affectionate, mutual, friendly and brotherly/sisterly. Christians should go so far as to eagerly compete with one another in order to outdo one another in manifesting and promoting the reciprocal respect and honoring of one another that is to be a hallmark of Christian love.

12:11 Beginning a powerful salvo of concise and spirited exhortations, Paul vigorously excites his readers not to allow their burning Christian zeal to wane or wither. They must rather remain intensely fervent in the Spirit as they persevere in serving the Lord.

b. Christians should love one another in, through and for hope.

12:12 While practicing love toward one another Christians are to rejoice in their sure and confident hope for God's future salvation. This hope enables Christians to persevere in their care and concern for one another. Painful distress or suffering need not interrupt, prevent or destroy Christian love, for it is part of Christian hope to "be steadfast in suffering" (see 5:3–4; 8:18–25, 35–37).

And the continual praying that Paul recommends is also part of hope's perseverance, as it empowers Christians to persist in their genuine love for one another. Since it is in prayer that Christians express their hope for the future completion of God's salvific will (see 8:26–27), being constant in prayer, by keeping them mindful of their hope for the future, spurs Christians on in their love for one another. Christians are to love one another, then, in and through the joy, steadfastness and prayer that accompany Christian hope for God's future salvation.

c. Christians should be caring, hospitable, compassionate and friendly toward all.

12:13 Paul entreats his Christian readers to share their material resources in order to alleviate the needs of other Christians, who are "saints" or "holy ones" of God. They will thereby be pursuing and practicing the hospitality that is part of authentic Christian love.

12:14 Christians are to extend their love even to enemies (see Matt 5:44; Luke 6:28; 1 Cor 4:12), by calling down God's blessing rather than a curse upon those who persecute them.

12:15 Christians should cultivate a love that is sensitive and compassionate to various situations. They should be capable of either rejoicing or weeping in sorrow with others when the occasion demands it.

12:16 Paul discourages his listeners from proud, individualistic aspirations or striving which could disrupt and divide the community. He bids them instead to associate with those who are lowly so as to demonstrate the same sincere, friendly and genuine love to all.

d. Christians should foster peace and never take revenge on others.

12:17 Turning to the theme of revenge, Paul urges his Christian audience to carefully think ahead and take every precaution toward what will make for agreeable and harmonious human relations before a conflict can develop. But when a conflict does arise, Christians should avoid the vicious circle of revenge by never repaying an "evil" act or injury with another evil act or injury.

12:18 As far as possible and to the extent that it depends upon them, Christians should take it upon themselves to promote and foster peaceable relations with all.

12:19 In view of their hope for God's future salvation of all (11:32) Christians should never avenge themselves. They should rather leave all retaliation to the manifestation of God's "wrath" in the future judgment, in accord with God's scriptural promise that he himself will be the one to execute vindication and take reprisal (Deut 32:35).

12:20 Calling upon the wise scriptural advice of Prov 25:21–22, Paul astounds and jolts his readers with the rather unusual admonition (but see Matt 5:44) that they should care for the needs even of their enemies, because of the possibility of thereby contributing to their conversion. For if Christians mercifully give food and drink to hungry and thirsty enemies, they will equivalently be "heaping burning coals" upon the heads of their enemies. And these figurative "burning coals" of mercy will hopefully ignite the remorse and repentance of the enemies to thereby bring about peace.

12:21 In a final thrust Paul encouragingly exhorts his audience not to allow themselves to be conquered by the evil or injury done to them. They should rather make every effort to conquer and overcome the evil or injury by faithfully practicing the "good" will of God (12:2, 9).

Paul propels his fellow Christians, then, to persistently perform the "good," the concrete will of God for the here and now, by extending the genuine love of care and concern to all, even to enemies, and thereby keep their Christian hope authentically open to the future salvation of God.

4. Romans 13:1–7:

1 Let every person submit to superior authorities. For there is no authority except from God, and those which exist have been instituted by God. 2 Therefore whoever opposes these authorities resists the order established by God, and those who resist will receive condemnation for themselves. 3 For rulers are not a terror to good conduct but to bad. Do you want to have no fear of authority? Do what is good, and you will have its praise. 4 For it is the servant of God for your good. But if you do what is bad, be afraid, for it does not bear the sword in vain; as the servant of God it is the executor for his wrath on one who does what is bad. 5 Therefore it is necessary to submit, not only because of the wrath but also for the sake of conscience. 6 For this reason you also pay taxes, since the authorities are ministers of God, occupying themselves with this very thing. 7 Pay to all their dues, the tax to whom the tax is due, the toll to whom the toll is due, respect to whom respect is due, honor to whom honor is due.

a. Everyone should submit to authority that has been instituted by God.

13:1 For their ultimate well-being Paul offers his readers the sage advice that everyone should submit to superior governing authorities. Since in Paul's view such governmental authority has been set up by

God himself to serve his purpose and order, acquiescing to ruling authorities is equivalent to obeying God himself.

13:2 Paul cautions that those who would defy these authorities would be withstanding the very order established and willed by God. They would jeopardize their cherished hope for God's future salvation, and could only look forward to dire despair, as "they will receive condemnation" rather than hoped for salvation in the judgment.

b. As God's servant ruling authority incites good conduct and deters the bad.

13:3–4 If his audience wishes to live with consciences free of the fear of ruling authorities, Paul, with friendly and sagacious counsel, recommends that they adhere to good conduct and shun the bad. They will then have nothing to be afraid of; indeed, they will then be praised by governing authority.

Ruling authority, which is actually God's servant, fosters the ultimate "good" of Paul's listeners by guiding and provoking them to good rather than bad behavior. If they were to act wrongly, they would then have cause to fear authority. For, as God's servant, governing authority has the responsibility and prerogative to administer God's furious "wrath" upon evildoers.

13:5 Therefore, it is entirely essential for Paul's auditors to comply with authority by doing the "good" now, God's "good" will for everyday living (12:2). Christians will then be promoting and maintaining their hope for God's future "good" and avoid living with a conscience plagued by terrifying dread of his future "wrath."

13:6–7 Likewise, for the sake of avoiding God's future "wrath" and living with a conscience free of anxiety, it is advisable for all Christians to cooperate with rulers, God's ministers even for collecting revenue, by dutifully paying them whatever taxes, tolls, respect and honor they deserve.

5. Romans 13:8–10:

8 Owe no one anything except to love one another; for the one who loves the other has fulfilled the Law. 9 For, "You shall not commit adultery, You shall not kill, You shall not steal, You shall not covet" (Exod 20:13–15 = Deut 5:17–19, 21), and any other commandment, are summed up in this word, "You shall love your neighbor as yourself" (Lev 19:18). 10 Love does no harm to a neighbor; love then is the fulfillment of the Law.

a. When Christians love one another they fulfill God's Law.

13:8 Here Paul brings his preceding exhortations regarding Christian love to a fitting climax. Playfully lingering on the notion of paying what one "owes" (13:6–7), Paul implores his readership not to "owe" a debt to anyone, except the debt of loving one another in the Christian community. Performing such love accomplishes what God intends in his Law.

b. To love rather than harm one's neighbor sums up all the other commandments of God's Law.

13:9 Such summary decalogue commandments as not committing adultery, killing, stealing and coveting, as well as any other possible commandment, are summed up by God's command from Lev 19:18 that everyone should have the same love for one's neighbor as for oneself.[2]

13:10 Christian love is such that it never does "evil" or harm to a neighbor, but rather effects the "good" (12:2, 9, 17; 13:3–4) that Paul has been exhorting for his readers as the way to live out their Christian hope for God's future "good." Love, the active care and concern for the other, achieves all that God's Law has ever commanded.

The fact that love fulfills God's Law, then, provides added incentive attracting Paul's readers to follow his persistent directive for mutual love to prevail in the Christian community.

6. Romans 13:11–14:

11 And be especially aware of the time; it is already the hour for you to wake from sleep, for now our salvation is closer than when we began to believe. 12 The night is far advanced, the day is at hand. Let us put off then the works of darkness, let us clothe ourselves with the armor of light. 13 In accord with the day let us walk properly, not in orgies and drunkenness, not in sexual excesses and debaucheries, not in rivalry and jealousy. 14 But clothe yourselves with the Lord Jesus Christ, and entertain no forethought to satisfy the appetites of the flesh.

a. The salvation that Christians hope for is always coming closer.

13:11 In accord with the apocalyptic-eschatological flavor of his thought Paul injects a strong dose of extreme urgency into his general exhortation for Christian communal love. Paul's preceding admonitions and injunctions centering on love and the "good" (12:1–13:10) acquire an even more serious and pressing tenor.

As the eschatological age has already dawned, Paul warns his Christian audience to be awake and alert to the time in which they are now living. The longed for end-time "salvation," which is the goal of our Christian hope (see 1:16; 5:9, 10; 8:24; 9:27; 10:1, 9, 10, 13; 11:11, 26), is relentlessly and inevitably coming closer to us than when we first started to believe.

13:12 Since the "night" of the old age is already far advanced and the "day" of the new age is luminously bursting through, it is most crucial and appropriate for us Christians to dismantle ourselves of the past, evil "works of darkness" and clothe ourselves with a new apparel, a new demeanor and conduct, the shining "armor of light," which combats the forces of moral wickedness. With this "clothing" metaphor to characterize one's behavior, Paul impresses upon his readers the necessity for them to wear and display a new mode of living.

b. The conduct of Christians should accord with their hope for salvation.

13:13 We Christians should now "walk," that is, act and behave, properly in accord with the light of the new "day" that has dawned. Paul reinforces his earlier plea that Christians not conform themselves to "this present age" but mold themselves and live in accord with their renewed way of thinking in their present situation of hope for future salvation (12:2).

This new Christian conduct excludes such moral degradation as orgies, drunkenness, sexual excesses and debaucheries, which is degenerate activity characteristic of the despair of the darkness of the night and inappropriate to the hope of the new daylight. Christians must also avoid rivalry and jealousy, conduct which especially disrupts and destroys Christian communal love.

13:14 In correspondence with the renewal of their minds Paul's listeners must eradicate any forethought about satisfying the ravenous desires of the old existence according to the "flesh." They would then slip and tumble back into the dark night of hopelessness (see 6:12; 7:7–25). They should rather keep themselves "clothed" with the Lord Jesus Christ by conducting themselves in accord with the hope that comes from their baptismal faith.

With an excited and decisive urgency Paul has instilled within his audience a sense of how absolutely imperative it is for them to exhibit moral comportment that is consonant with our Christian hope for the future "salvation" that is drawing ever closer.

B. Rom 14:1–15:13: The "Strong" in Faith Should Show Christian Love toward the "Weak" in Faith.

Continuing his parenesis Paul addresses a specific problem within the Roman Christian community. He focuses his exhortatory thrust upon the Christian love and peace that should prevail between two distinct groups of Christians at Rome, those whom Paul designates the "strong" as opposed to the "weak" in faith.

Although Paul does not fully disclose the precise details behind this rift, it quite possibly has its origins and background in certain problems caused by idolatrous pagan practices within the Roman cultural milieu.

At least part of the problem at Rome seems to be similar to the one Paul addressed at Corinth (see 1 Cor 8–10). Many Christians, the so-called "weak" in faith, had scruples or weak consciences about eating food sold in market places after it had been cultically dedicated to the idols in pagan temples. In addition to abstaining from meat considered "unclean" (14:2, 14) and from wine (14:21), the "weak" in faith at Rome practiced an observance of certain days (14:5–6). These Christians may have been primarily but not exclusively those with a Jewish heritage.

The so-called "strong" in faith were those Christians who had no scruples about eating food which had been offered to idols. They had a strong faith since they knew and were convinced that idols had no real existence and that there is only one God (1 Cor 8:4). They considered themselves superior to the "weak" whose troubled consciences prevented them from risking possible association with idolatrous worship. These "strong" in faith were not exclusively Gentile Christians; Paul included himself among them (14:14; 15:1).[3]

1. Romans 14:1–12:

1 Welcome one who is weak in faith, but not for the deciding of disputes. 2 One believes he may eat anything, while he who is weak eats only vegetables. 3 Let not the one who eats despise the one who abstains, and let not one who abstains pass judgment on one who eats, for God has welcomed him. 4 Who are you to judge another's servant? It is before his own Lord that he stands or falls. And he will be upheld, for the Lord has the power to make him stand.

5 One regards one day over another, while another regards every day the same. Let each one be fully convinced in his own

mind. 6 Whoever observes a certain day, observes it in honor of the Lord; and whoever eats something, eats it in honor of the Lord, for he gives thanks to God. Likewise, whoever refuses to eat something, refuses to eat it in honor of the Lord and gives thanks to God.

7 None of us lives for himself only, and none of us dies for himself only. 8 For if we live, we live for the Lord, and if we die, we die for the Lord. So whether we live or die, then, we belong to the Lord. 9 For Christ died and came to life again in order to establish his lordship over both the dead and the living. 10 You, then—why do you judge your brother? And you—why do you despise your brother? For we shall all stand before the judgment seat of God; 11 as it is written, "As I live, says the Lord (Isa 49:18), every knee shall bow to me, and every tongue shall praise God" (Isa 45:23). 12 So then, each of us will give account of himself to God.

a. Christians should welcome and not despise or judge one another.

14:1 With the plural address directed to his readers as a Christian community, Paul entreats them not to exclude but to fully "welcome" or "accept" into their midst those whom they may consider to be "weak" in faith. Christians who are "strong" in faith should welcome these fellow Christians and accept them along with their peculiar "weakness"; they should not, then, dispute or argue with them about the particular convictions of their conscience.

14:2 There are some Christians whose faith allows them to eat even the food which others deem to be unclean, possibly because of its prior use in idolatrous cults. But some other Christians, whose consciences may be considered "weaker" in this matter, think it is better simply to eat vegetables and to avoid eating meat altogether, rather than risk the eating of what they regard as unclean because of its possible use in idolatrous rituals. They would thereby scrupulously avoid any participation in or association with the worship of idols.

14:3 Those Christians whose consciences permit them to eat what others abstain from eating should not scornfully look down upon or despise those who refuse to eat. And conversely, those Christians who cautiously refrain from eating what may be contaminated should not judge or condemn those who have no scruples about so eating. After all, God himself has already welcomed and accepted such a person as a believing Christian. And so Paul's readers should surely welcome and accept what God has already welcomed and accepted, namely, one another as fellow believing Christians.

14:4 Reverting to the diatribal device of interrogating an imaginary interlocutor, Paul warns his listeners against presumptuously taking over the prerogative of passing judgment on another Christian. That responsibility belongs exclusively and totally to one's Lord and Master. In the last judgment a Christian will stand or fall not before another Christian, but solely before his own Lord. And Paul assures his audience that the Lord has sufficient power to uphold and thus bring his "servant" through the judgment.

b. Every Christian must follow the full conviction of his conscience.

14:5 There are some Christians who single out certain days in the calendar for special religious observance, while others regard all days equally. In any case, what is important is that each of Paul's Christian auditors faithfully follows the dictates of his own mind and conscience.

14:6 Serving, honoring and praising God transcends the differences in the convictions of Christians. A Christian who follows the conviction of his mind by specially observing a certain day serves and honors the Lord. Those who obey their consciences by choosing to eat meat which may have been offered to idols, as well as those who likewise follow their convictions by avoiding such food, honor the Lord and render thanks and praise to God. In this case, then, God can be fittingly honored both by eating and by not eating the food in question.

Paul wants his readership to realize that it does not really matter to God whether a Christian eats the food in question or not. What is important, however, is whether a Christian remains true to the full conviction of his/her mind and thereby properly serves his/her Lord and God.

c. Christians should not judge one another since we will all be judged by God.

14:7–8 A Christian does not live or die for himself or herself only, but lives and dies in complete and total dedication to the one and same Lord of us all (see 6:8–11). Both while we are alive and when we die, then, we belong entirely to the Lord.

14:9 Christ died and came to life again through his resurrection precisely in order to initiate his mighty rule over all of us, not only after we have died, but now, while we are still living.

14:10 In the diatribal style Paul indicts imaginary representatives of the two distinct Christian groups he has been addressing. Those who are "weak" in faith and thus do not eat should not judge or condemn their fellow Christians who are "strong" in faith and thus do eat.

Likewise, the "strong" in faith must not disdain or despise their fellow Christians who are "weak" in faith (see 14:3–4).

Paul's Christian audience should rather leave the activity of judging others in the hands of God where it belongs, for all without exception will stand before the judgment seat of God. There is no need then for Christians to exercise judgment on one another.

14:11 Paul's scriptural testimony to reinforce this point emphatically underscores the exclusive right of God himself and no other to sovereignly judge all persons: "As *I* live, says the *Lord,* every knee shall bow to *me,* and every tongue shall praise *God.*" God and not human beings will render judgment on all.

14:12 As further motivation for Christians to refrain from judging and condemning the fully convinced conduct of other fellow Christians, Paul pointedly cautions his readership to keep in mind that each individual, whether "strong" or "weak," will have to give account of his or her own conduct and way of living to God in the final judgment.

By persuading his listeners to leave judgment of others entirely to the future of God, Paul continues his overall exhortation for Christian love in terms of the mutual respect and consideration that is to prevail within the Christian community, even among Christians with quite diverse and contrary but sincere and honest opinions and practices.

2. *Romans 14:13–23:*

13 Let us then no longer judge one another. But rather decide this: not to place an obstacle or hindrance before a fellow Christian. 14 I know and am convinced in the Lord Jesus that nothing is unclean of itself; but if someone considers something to be unclean, it is unclean for that person. 15 For if through food your fellow Christian is grieved, you are no longer acting from love. Cease destroying with your food one for whom Christ died!

16 Do not let your good be defamed! 17 For the kingdom of God is not a matter of eating and drinking but of righteousness and peace and joy in the Holy Spirit. 18 And whoever serves Christ in this way is pleasing to God and esteemed by human beings. 19 So then let us pursue what makes for peace and the edification of one another.

20 Do not, for the sake of food, destroy the work of God! All food is indeed clean, but it is wrong for someone to eat because of scandal. 21 What is right is not to eat meat or drink wine or do anything which makes your fellow Christian stumble. 22 Keep the faith you have in this matter between yourself and God. Blessed is one who does

not need to reproach himself for doing what he approves. 23 But one who has doubts stands condemned, if he eats, because he is not then acting from faith. For whatever is not based on faith is sin.

a. For the sake of love Christians must not let their convictions be a cause of scandal and harm to fellow Christians.

14:13 Paul exhorts the Christian community at Rome to stop judging one another regarding this particular problem of eating food which may have been offered to idols. Especially the "strong" in faith among Paul's audience should take care not to hinder or scandalize a fellow Christian by eating this food and thus causing this "weak" Christian to stumble in his faith.

14:14 Paul includes himself with the "strong" in faith on this matter. He himself is fully convinced from his union with the Lord Jesus that nothing is "unclean" of itself. But it does become unclean for anyone who thinks it unclean. And those who know and are convinced that nothing is unclean must respect this.

14:15 With a shift to the second person singular Paul addresses each "strong" Christian among his readers individually: If a fellow Christian is grieved because of what "you" eat, then the Christian love (*agape*), the mutual concern and respect, that should prevail in the community would be sadly lacking.

"You," the "strong" in faith, should take it upon yourself not to "destroy" with mere food one to whom Christ dearly extended his love by dying. In other words, "you" who are "strong" in faith must take care that your conduct of eating food does not destroy a fellow Christian's faith and hope for the salvation that comes from the death of Christ.

b. The pursuit for the peace and edification of the Christian community should transcend differences of conviction.

14:16 Shifting back to the second person plural, Paul exhorts the Christian community as a whole not to let the "good" (see 12:2, 9, 21; 13:3–4) they accomplish in accord with God's will by loving one another be defamed and misconstrued by others as something that is bad.

14:17 The kingdom of God is not to be ridiculously reduced to such a relatively trivial matter as the eating or drinking of certain foods. Rather, the kingdom of God means that God's salvific benefits of "righteousness" and "peace" and "joy" are to reign in the Christian community through the Holy Spirit.

14:18 In this matter of "food" and "drink" the one who serves

Christ in accord with the righteousness, peace and joy now available in and through the Holy Spirit lives the new life of Christian hope as one "pleasing" (see 12:1–2) to God and approvingly esteemed, rather than "defamed" (14:16), by others.

14:19 Therefore, as Paul sums up, we Christians should live already in the kingdom of God for which we hope by pursuing and striving after those things that foster peace and mutual edification within the community.

c. Christians must not let a matter of eating and drinking destroy the faith of fellow Christians.

14:20 Reverting again to the second person singular, Paul implores the individual "strong" Christian not to destroy the "work of God," the joyous peace and harmony of the community that results from mutual edification, for the sake of mere food. Although all food may be considered ritually "clean" and able to be safely consumed, it is bad for a Christian who has a "weak" conscience in this matter to eat what he regards as "unclean" due to the scandal given when a "strong" Christian eats the food in question.

14:21 It is good for the well-being of the Christian community, then, for the "strong" Christian not to eat the meat or drink the wine in question, nor to do anything else that will make a fellow Christian stumble in his faith.

14:22 The untroubled conscience and freedom in faith that "you," the "strong" Christian, possess regarding such food you should keep as a private matter strictly between yourself and God, so as not to scandalize a "weak" fellow Christian. Then you will be blessed by God as you will not need to scrutinize or reproach yourself for creating possible scandal by doing something you have absolutely no qualms of conscience about doing. In this way you will not destroy the conviction of the "weak."

14:23 For if one who is "weak" eats in doubt he thereby loses his conviction as well as his future hope for salvation, since he then stands already "condemned." Such a doubtful eating, because not proceeding from faith, would plunge one back into the hopeless situation of sin.

Paul thus urges his Christian readers not to demolish another's faith and hope by their own conduct, even when that conduct proceeds from their own strong conviction in faith. Rather, they should show a genuine concern and respect for the consciences of their fellow Christians.

3. Romans 15:1–6:

1 We who are strong ought to bear the weaknesses of the weak and not please ourselves. 2 Let each of us please his neighbor for edification to bring about what is good. 3 For Christ did not please himself; but as it is written, "The insults of those who insulted you fell upon me" (Ps 69:10). 4 For whatever was written beforehand was written for our instruction, that by steadfastness and by the encouragement of the scriptures we might have hope. 5 May the God of steadfastness and encouragement grant you to think among yourselves in the same way, according to Christ Jesus, 6 so that together with one voice you may glorify the God and Father of our Lord Jesus Christ!

a. Strong Christians ought to bear with weak Christians for the edification and good of the community.

15:1 Paul advises the "strong" Christians, among whom he includes himself, that precisely because they are the stronger members of the community they ought to rely upon and utilize this strength to bear with the weak consciences of the "weak." The "strong" ought to actively "endure" or "bear," and not simply tolerate, the scruples of their weaker fellow Christians as part of the general obligation of Christian love.[4]

In other words, the "strong" ought not to "please" themselves by eating the meat which the scrupulous "weak" are convinced is unclean. Such conduct would violate the Christian love, the respect and concern, that should prevail in the community (see 14:15).

15:2 Paul extends his exhortation involving "pleasing" to each and every member of his audience. Each of us, the "strong" as well as the "weak," must exercise love by pleasing his fellow Christian and thus promoting mutual edification to bring about what is the "good," the salvific will of God (12:2, 9, 17, 21; 13:3–4, 10; 14:16), for the Christian community.[5]

15:3 That Christ "did not please himself" should motivate the "strong" not to please themselves and each member of the community to please his neighbor. Paul illustrates that Christ did not please himself by citing Psalm 69:10 as words uttered by Christ in the context of his passion and death, so that the "insults" are those of enemies against God, which have now fallen upon Christ. Thus, in exhorting his listeners to Christian love by "pleasing" the other, Paul appeals to the love of Christ for us as manifested by his passion and death in accord with the scriptural plan of God.

b. It is through steadfastness and encouragement that we maintain our Christian hope.

15:4 Paul draws out the significance not only of the previous scriptural quotation but of all the scriptures, which have relevance for the present age in terms of the instruction they offer us for the daily situations of Christian living (see 4:22–24; 1 Cor 9:10; 10:11).

He then arrives at the goal of his previous exhortation to love (15:1–2) and of the instruction offered by the scriptures (15:3): It is by "steadfastness" and the "encouragement" of the scriptures that we Christians "have," that is, "maintain," "preserve" or "keep" our hope. Here Paul makes the relationship between Christian love and hope more explicit for his audience. The point of intersection between hope and love resides in "steadfastness," which is essential to Christian love (15:1–6) and which also produces (5:3–4) and preserves hope.

"Steadfastness" or persevering "endurance" describes the attitude of Christ in not pleasing himself but rather taking upon himself and bearing the insults directed against God (15:3). Such "steadfastness" is necessary for the "strong" not to please themselves but to bear the weaknesses of the "weak" (15:1), and for all Christians to please their neighbor for the peaceful and harmonious good of the community (15:2). Hence, "steadfastness" is essential to the exercise of Christian love.

And Paul has previously illustrated for his readers how "steadfastness" is also an attribute of Christian hope (5:3–4; 8:25; 12:12), as it expresses the persevering endurance that a Christian must actively put forth in the face of suffering as he awaits the hoped for future completion of God's salvific activity. In the midst of suffering, hope assumes the form of "steadfastness," which, in turn produces new hope (see 5:3–4).

Paul thus persuades his readers that we Christians who, "by steadfastness," persevere in our love toward one another so that the salvific will of God is accomplished for the community (15:2) *thereby* maintain our "hope" of sharing in the future and final completion of God's salvation.

Coupled with "steadfastness" as a means for maintaining hope is the "encouragement" of the scriptures. The word for "encouragement" (*paraklesis*) carries with it a connotation of "comfort" or "consolation."

That the will of God was accomplished through the love of Christ in enduring the ignominious insults of enemies for the sake of God (15:3) gives Paul's Christian auditors the encouragement and comfort that the will of God for the good of the community will likewise be achieved through their love of one another (15:1–2). The encouragement and comfort that arises from God's scriptural instruction, then, helps us Christians in the midst of our daily living to keep and maintain our hope for God's future.

15:5–6 Paul strongly reinforces his exhortation with the authoritative weight of his own personal prayer-wish.[6] He prays that God may bestow upon his Christian audience the steadfastness and encouragement they need to regard one another in the same way as Christ has regarded them, that is, to exercise the loving concern to which Paul has just urged them: They are not to "please" themselves (15:1) but to "please" their neighbor (15:2), just as Christ did not "please" himself (15:3).[7]

The result will be a harmoniously unified Christian community, so that together with one voice "you," the diverse Christian community including "strong" and "weak," may glorify the God and Father of our Lord Jesus Christ. This very unity, in itself, as an accomplishment of God's will for the community, is what "glorifies" and gives praise to God. In order for the Christian community to praise and "glorify" God as a liturgical assembly, Paul prays that they create the unity that emerges from their steadfast pursuit and performance of Christian love. And if we can "glorify" God in and through the exercise of the mutual respect and loving concern that unifies us as a Christian community, then we are *thereby* preserving our hope (15:4) for the future and final "glory" of God (see 5:2).

4. *Romans 15:7–13:*

7 Welcome one another, therefore, because Christ welcomed you, for the glory of God. 8 For I declare that Christ became a servant of the circumcision for the sake of God's fidelity, to confirm the promises to the patriarchs, 9 and that the Gentiles might glorify God for the sake of mercy, as it is written,

> "Therefore I will praise you among the Gentiles,
> and sing to your name." (Ps 18:49)

10 And again it is said,
> "Rejoice, O Gentiles, with his people!" (Deut 32:43)

11 And again,

"Praise, all you Gentiles, the Lord,
and let all peoples acclaim him!" (Ps 117:1)

12 And again Isaiah says,

"The root of Jesse will come,
he who arises to rule the Gentiles,
in him the Gentiles will hope." (Isa 11:10)

13 May the God of hope fill you with complete joy and peace in believing, so that you may abound in hope by the power of the Holy
Spirit!

a. The Christian community of Jews and Gentiles should actualize their unity by welcoming one another as Christ has welcomed them.

15:7 Paul's exhortation moves beyond the specific rift between
the "strong" and the "weak" to the more general situation of the Christian community as composed of Jews and Gentiles. He beseeches his
Christian readership to warmly welcome and accept one another because Christ himself has welcomed both Jews and Gentiles to further
the glory of God. By so welcoming one another as part of Christian
love for the "glory of God," the future goal of Christian hope (5:2;
8:18, 24–25), Jewish and Gentile Christians may thereby maintain
their cherished hope for future salvation (15:4).

15:8 With a touch of solemnity Paul reminds his readers that
Christ became a servant of the "circumcision," that is, of the Jews, for
the sake of continuing to manifest God's well-known and ever enduring "fidelity" or "faithfulness" to his people.

Christ demonstrated God's ongoing fidelity by confirming the
powerful promises pronounced to Israel's patriarchs of old. Being a
Jew Christ not only fulfilled the ancient promises that the Messiah
would come from the Jews (see 1:2–3; 9:5; 15:12), but he also thereby
"confirmed" or "made valid" the yet-to-be fulfilled promises uttered
to the Jewish patriarchs for God's future salvation (see 9:4–5; 3:1–2;
4:13–25). In other words, by becoming a servant of the Jews Christ
made possible the future fulfillment of the promises pronounced to
the Jewish patriarchs, so that these powerful promises may continue
to inspire and awaken hope for the future salvation of God.[8]

15:9 But Christ became a servant of the Jews also in order that
the Gentiles might glorify God for the sake of his mercy. That Christ

has enabled the ancient promises to remain strong and valid for the sake of God's enduring "fidelity" to the Jews means that now the Gentiles can also "glorify" God for the sake of his marvelous "mercy." "Fidelity" (*aletheia*) and "mercy" (*eleos*) are often coupled in the Old Testament as a unity to describe God's salvific dealings on behalf of his people and thus serve to illustrate the unity and mutuality of Jews and Gentiles here.[9]

By perceptively and cleverly demonstrating how Christ has already "welcomed" both the Jews and Gentiles among his audience, Paul persuasively prods his readers to continue to play their respective and essential roles in "glorifying God" by warmly "welcoming" one another in Christian love for the sake of God's glory (15:7), the future aim of their hope.

15:9–11 That there can and must be a mutual respect and concern between Jews and Gentiles for the glory of God Paul dazzlingly illustrates with a striking and dramatically constructed series of scriptural citations (15:9–12) meticulously woven together by a repeated occurrence of the word "Gentiles" and by various depictions of "glorifying" God.

Whereas the first quotation (Ps 18:49) vibrantly portrays the praise of God by a Jew among Gentiles, the second quotation (Deut 32:43) directly addresses the Gentiles and excitedly invites them to rejoice along with God's people, Israel. The third quote (Ps 117:1) universalizes the invitation to "*all* the Gentiles" and to "*all* the peoples" to praise the Lord, the God of Israel. These stunning scriptural promises prompt the praise of God and exemplify how the Gentiles "glorify" God for the sake of his mercy. They encompass both Jewish and Gentile Christians in the global praising and glorifying of God.

With these electrifying scriptural invitations Paul encouragingly exhorts his Christian listeners to sincerely welcome and openly accept one another as part of Christian love. And they aptly exhibit "the encouragement of the scriptures" through which Christians preserve and maintain their hope (15:4) by their continual respect and concern, their Christian love, toward one another.

b. By mutual love we Christians may all abound in hope.

15:12 The fourth and final citation (Isa 11:10) pronounces the prophetic promise that the "sprout of Jesse," the Messiah, will come from the Jews and extend his rule over the Gentiles, so that in him the Gentiles "will hope." This dramatic apex to the lively series of scriptural quotes most explicitly illuminates how Christ has fulfilled and confirmed the promises made to the Jewish patriarchs (15:8), so that they continue to ignite and stir the fervent hope of Christians.

Having become a servant of the Jews (15:8) Christ has fulfilled the prophetic promise for a "sprout of Jesse," a Jewish Messiah, who would also reign over the Gentiles. Christ has thus "confirmed" this promise as a strong foundation and springboard for further hope, so that its promise that the Gentiles "will hope" in him may now be fulfilled by Paul's Christian audience cordially "welcoming" one another in love (15:7).

Paul has persistently implored his readers to the mutual exercise of Christian love precisely so that they may have and maintain their Christian hope (15:4). The harmonious unity, peace and mutual respect that is to prevail in the Christian community establishes, preserves and assures their Christian hope for the future of God.

15:13 Reaching the pinnacle of his encouraging exhortations, Paul climactically reinforces and sums up his preceding parenesis with a zestful and zealous prayer for its accomplishment. Releasing a closing burst of burning enthusiasm, he invokes God as the "God of hope," that is, as the ultimate source and giver of hope. He prays that the God who awakens and sustains hope may fill his Christian readers with complete "joy" and "peace" in their life of faith.

"Joy" characterizes the lusty "glorifying" of God that is colorfully depicted in terms of rejoicing and praising in the above scriptural citations (15:9–11), and that results when Christians love one another. And "peace" refers to the unity and harmony (15:6) that is effected by Christian love.

This joy and peace which the God of hope copiously bestows upon Paul's audience when they love one another results in a fertile growth and rampant increase of hope so that their Christian hope richly "abounds" or "overflows" (see 5:15, 17). And this marvelous superabundance of hope springs from the power of the Holy Spirit, whose essential role in the dynamics of Christian hope has already been illustrated (5:5; 8:23–27).

With this final and prayerful thrust of encouragement Paul enthralls his listeners with the realization that as Christians they can never have enough hope. Christian hope never stagnates or stands still; it can and must continually, vibrantly and prosperously grow until it lushly and lavishly "abounds."

C. Summary

Paul has exhorted and encouraged his audience to cultivate and foster a mutual and communal Christian "love," a sincere respect and concern for one another, both in their general everyday living (12:1–13:14) and in view of a peculiar problem involving divergent convictions and fundamental differences among fellow Christians (14:1–15:13).

In light of their new Christian way of life (12:1–2) as well as their ever approaching future hope (13:11–14), Paul has earnestly urged his readers to live in Christian love of one another (13:8–10). The varied charisms given by God to certain individuals for the benefit and edification of the Christian community should be performed in loving concern and respect of fellow Christians (12:3–8).

For the sake of the peace and harmony of the community Paul's Christian auditors should humbly submit to the governing authorities (13:1–7) and not take revenge on enemies (12:17–21) nor judge one another (14:1–12). And Christians must take care lest they destroy a fellow Christian with their own convictions (14:13–23).

Paul has entreated his Christian listeners to love one another with persevering steadfastness in order to maintain and promote their profound hope for the future of God (12:9–16; 15:4–5). They may keep and preserve this confident hope with the aid of the instruction offered by the scriptures, which inspire in Christians an attitude of "encouragement" and "comfort" so that they are able to love one another as Christ loved them. For when Christians, through steadfastness and encouragement, love one another, they glorify God, thus promoting the "glory of God," and thereby maintain their strong hope for the future and final "glory of God" (15:1–12).

Through the persuasiveness of his own intercessory prayers Paul has prodded his audience to so strive for Christian care and concern, mutual love, that God may fill them with complete joy and peace so that their stalwart Christian hope may steadily increase and splendidly abound. By their Christian love, then, Paul's readers not only maintain their constant hope but enable it to increase and grow. But it is God himself who generously gives the steadfastness and encouragement that establishes, preserves and promotes Christian hope; it is he who continually boosts hope until it joyously overflows. Pursuing the peace, unity and harmony of the community by loving one another, based upon Christ's love for them, allows Christians not only to keep and preserve hope but to richly abound in their hope for God's future salvation (15:4–6, 13).

In accord with his design for the Letter (see 1:11–12) Paul has continued to encourage and awaken the hope of his readers. In Romans 1–8 Paul confidently proclaimed and demonstrated the absolutely assured hope that Christians may have for the future glory and salvation of God. In Romans 9–11 Paul increased this hope as he broadened its horizon to embrace the hope that *all* Israel will be saved, so that Christians may securely hope in God's merciful salvation of *all*.

And in Romans 12:1–15:13 Paul has applied the splendid hope he previously pronounced and exhibited in Romans 1–11 to daily and critical situations of Christian living. He persistently propelled his readership to live out the hope that is now theirs by sincerely loving one another in order not only to preserve but to abundantly enlarge their hope for the future and final salvation of God.

When we listen to the prayer of Paul (15:13), which serves as the noble pinnacle for the entire Letter's argumentation and persuasion, keeping in mind his stated intention of encouraging his readers to share in the hope springing from faith (1:11–12), it aptly epitomizes the exciting and vivacious theme of Christian hope dominating the Letter: "May the God of *hope* fill you with complete joy and peace in believing, so that you may *abound in hope* by the power of the Holy Spirit!"

NOTES

1. For similar Pauline expressions of "newness" or "renewal" in Christian living, see 2 Cor 4:16; 5:17; Gal 6:15.

2. See also Gal 5:14; Matt 5:43; 19:18–19; Mark 12:31; Luke 10:27; Jas 2:8.

3. For other suggestions about the background of the problem between the "strong" and the "weak," see C. E. B. Cranfield, *Romans: A Shorter Commentary* (Grand Rapids: Eerdmans, 1985) 335–339.

4. Note Rom 13:8: "Owe no one anything, except to love one another . . ."

5. On the idea of love "edifying" or building up the Christian community elsewhere in Paul, see 1 Cor 8:1. And for notions similar to that of Rom 15:2, see 1 Cor 10:23–24; 10:33–11:1.

6. See G. P. Wiles, *Paul's Intercessory Prayers. The Significance of the Intercessory Prayer Passages in the Letters of St. Paul* (SNTSMS 24; Cambridge: Cambridge University Press, 1974) 79–83.

7. "Thinking the same toward one another" is also part of genuine Christian love in 12:16.

8. Recall how the "promise" God granted to the patriarch Abraham stimulates hope for the future (4:13–25).

9. For God's "mercy" toward the Gentiles, see Rom 9:15, 16, 23; 11:31–32.

Chapter VIII

Romans 15:14–16:27

Having successfully completed his bold presentation of the gospel of hope of which he is "not ashamed" (1:16–15:13), Paul concludes his great Letter to the Romans by returning to the theme of his "apostolic hope" of spreading the gospel to all nations (15:14–21) (see 1:5, 13–15). Paul's spirited presentation of the gospel in the Letter itself has already fulfilled part of his apostolic hope (1:14–15), namely, the strengthening and encouraging of the Christian hope of his Roman audience (1:11–12), who already believe in the gospel (1:8).

But in concluding the Letter Paul explains the important role the Christians at Rome are yet to play in his apostolic hope for the future of his missionary activity (15:22–33). He closes with cordial personal greetings and recommendations for those he knows in Rome because of their previous association with his evangelizing apostolate (16:1–16). A final exhortation is included (16:17–20), and after a final greeting (16:21–23) a summarizing doxology ends the Letter on a rousing high note (16:25–27).

A. Rom 15:14–21: Paul's Past Apostolic Success and Future Apostolic Hope.

Paul explains why it is that he has written so boldly in this Letter to his fellow Christians at Rome:

1. Romans 15:14–21:

14 I myself am convinced about you, my fellow Christians, that indeed you yourselves are full of goodness, filled with all knowledge, and capable of advising one another. 15 But I have written quite boldly to you in part, so as to remind you, because of the grace given

162

me by God 16 to be a minister of Christ Jesus to the nations, serving the gospel of God like a priest, so that the offering of the nations might be acceptable, consecrated in the Holy Spirit.

17 In Christ Jesus, then, I have reason for boasting of my work for God. 18 For I will not dare to speak of anything other than what Christ has accomplished through me for the obedience of the nations, by word and deed, 19 by the power of signs and wonders, by the power of the Spirit, so that from Jerusalem and as far round as Illyricum I have fully completed the preaching of the gospel of Christ, 20 thus making it a point to evangelize not where Christ has already been named, so as not to build on the foundation of another, 21 but as it is written,

"Those who have never been told of him will see,
and those who have never heard will understand." (Isa 52:15)

a. Paul has boldly written to the Roman Christians because they are part of his apostolate to all nations.

15:14 At the beginning of the Letter Paul had acknowledged that the faith of the Christians at Rome was well known throughout the world (1:8). Continuing in that vein, he assures his fellow Christian readers that he has written the preceding part of the Letter not because of any personal doubt he has about the maturity of their faith. Since they are full of goodness and knowledge, they are certainly capable of admonishing and directing their own Christian lives.

15:15 Nevertheless, Paul has written rather boldly, at least in part of the Letter, in order to remind his Christian audience at Rome of the gospel they already know and believe in. He is entitled to do this because of his God-given apostolate to preach the gospel to all nations (1:14–15). And so, even though his Roman audience are already firm Christian believers, Paul includes them within the purview of his world-wide evangelizing mission. He has reminded them of the gospel (1:16–15:13) they already believe in because they are part of the nations to whom he has been sent and authorized as an apostle by God.

15:16 With cultic imagery Paul describes his dedication to his task and privilege of preaching the gospel to all: He is a devoted "minister" of Christ Jesus to the nations, who serves the gospel of God like a "priest" assigned to perform worship in the Temple, so that the "offering" or "sacrifice" which consists in the various nations coming to faith in the gospel might be "acceptable" or "pleasing" to God, "consecrated" or "sanctified" by the Holy Spirit.

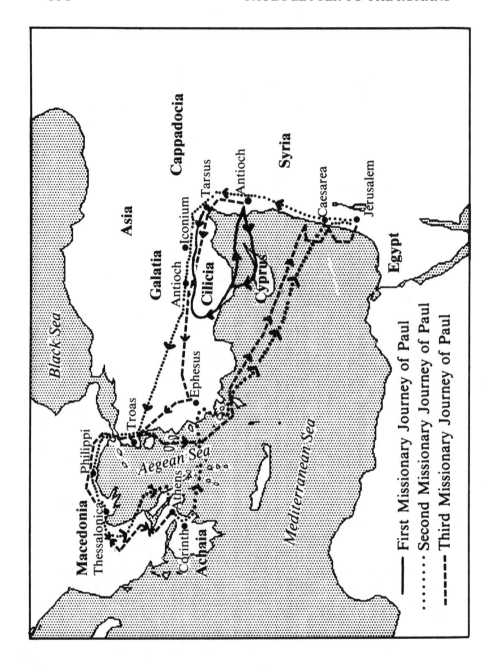

b. Christ has enabled Paul to successfully preach the gospel from Jerusalem as far as Illyricum.

15:17–19 Paul has ample reason to "boast" before God of his past achievements in preaching the gospel. This apostolic "boasting" emerges from what the risen Christ has already accomplished through Paul in bringing nations to the "obedience" of believing in the gospel through Paul's words and deeds, through the signs and wonders he has been empowered to perform by God's Spirit.

Paul is thus attracting his readership into his apostolic enterprise as he impresses them with how the "power" of God's Spirit has enabled him to spread the gospel of Christ to its "full completion," to have its full salvific effect, throughout the entire eastern Mediterranean region—from Jerusalem all the way to Illyricum (in present day Yugoslavia).

c. Paul has the apostolic hope of continuing to preach the gospel to those who have not yet heard it.

15:20–21 What God's power has already remarkably accomplished through Paul ignites and inflames his apostolic hope for the future spreading of the gospel. He ambitiously aspires to evangelize not where Christ has already been made known, so as not to interfere by building on the foundation laid by another evangelist, but rather to evangelize those who have not yet heard about Christ so that they may arrive at faith by "seeing" and "understanding." Paul's earnest hope for the future is that the prophetic promise of Isaiah 52:15 might be fulfilled through his preaching of the gospel. He hopes that those who have never been told of Christ "will see," and that those who have never heard of him "will understand."

Paul wants his Roman audience to feel and share in the excitement of his apostolic hope for the future expansion of the gospel, since they are to contribute significantly to it.

B. Rom 15:22–33: The Role of the Roman Christians in Paul's Future Apostolate.

Although Paul has presented the gospel in the Letter (see 1:15–16) as a substitute for his personal presence, now that he has finished his missionary activity in the regions from Jerusalem to Illyricum, he still longs to come in person to the Romans and hopes to visit them on his way to spreading the gospel as far as Spain.

1. Romans 15:22–33:

22 This is the reason I have so many times been prevented from coming to you. 23 But now, no longer having room for work in these regions, and for many years having had the longing to come to you, 24 I hope to see you in passing on my way to Spain, and to be sent on my way there by you, once I have enjoyed your company for a while.

25 Now, however, I am going to Jerusalem in service to the saints. 26 For Macedonia and Achaia have resolved to make some contribution for the poor among the saints at Jerusalem. 27 They have resolved to do it, and indeed they are indebted to them, for if the Gentiles have shared in their spiritual blessings, they are also indebted to minister to them in material blessings. 28 When I have finished this and delivered to them this benefit, I will go on by way of you to Spain. 29 And I know that when I come to you I will come in the fullness of the blessing of Christ.

30 I exhort you, fellow Christians, through our Lord Jesus Christ and through the love inspired by the Spirit, to strive together with me in your prayers to God on my behalf, 31 that I may be rescued from the unbelievers in Judea and my service for Jerusalem be acceptable to the saints, 32 so that as I come to you in joy by the will of God I may be refreshed together with you. 33 The God of peace be with you all! Amen.

a. Paul hopes to visit and be aided by the Roman Christians on his way to Spain.

15:22 Paul draws his Christian audience at Rome more deeply into his global missionary program. He wants them to realize that it has been his important apostolic responsibility of spreading the gospel through God's power to those who have not yet heard of Christ (15:17–21) that has many times hindered him from fulfilling his eager "longing" to come in person to the Christians at Rome.

15:23–24 Having successfully preached the gospel in the regions from Jerusalem to Illyricum, Paul still has a yearning desire to visit the Roman Christians and ardently hopes to do so on his way to Spain.

Paul has thus reached a major turning point in his magnificent missionary career: His success through the power of God in the eastern Mediterranean area has aroused his hope of bringing the gospel as far as Spain in the western Mediterranean region. And his Christian audience at Rome represent a strategic point in that exciting and ambitious endeavor.

The Christian community at Rome can play a pivotal part in this apostolic hope when Paul finally succeeds in coming to them. They can helpfully send him on his journey to Spain with such material support as food, money and companions,[1] after he has been spiritually satisfied and edified by their company for a while.

So, whereas Paul wrote the Letter with the explicit intention of spiritually "strengthening" and "encouraging" (1:11–12) his fellow Christians at Rome by proclaiming the sure hope they may have through their firm faith in the gospel (1:16–15:13), in his future visit with them, it is his Roman Christian audience who can support, encourage and increase Paul's apostolic hope of advancing the gospel to Spain. Thus will Paul and the Roman Christians be "*mutually* encouraged" (1:12)—the Romans by the Letter and Paul by the visit.

b. Paul must deliver the collection of the Christians at Macedonia and Achaia to the poor at Jerusalem.

15:25–26 But before Paul can satisfy his apostolic hope of going to Spain with the gospel by way of his visit to Rome, he must first fulfill yet another part of his apostolic hope—that of delivering the contribution collected by the Gentile Christians of Macedonia and Achaia to the poor among the Christians in Jerusalem.

15:27 With good reason Paul impresses upon his readers how the mother community at Jerusalem retains a very special significance with regard to the gospel. He has already demonstrated for his listeners how the Gentile Christians share in the "spiritual blessings" that have originated from Jerusalem, above all, in the gospel of hope based on the great promises given Israel (see 1:1–2; 3:2; 9–11; 15:7–12). The exquisite Christian hope the Gentiles now possess is founded on their faith in the gospel which originated from Jerusalem, so that the Gentiles are all the more indebted to serve the Jerusalem community in "material blessings."

And so Paul has fittingly capped off the concerted theme of the unity of Christian Jews and Gentiles running through the Letter to the Romans:

THE UNITY OF CHRISTIAN JEWS AND GENTILES

1:16:   For I am not ashamed of the gospel: It is the power of God for salvation to all who believe, to Jew first but also to Greek.

3:29–30:   Or is God the God of the Jews only? Is he not the God of Gentiles also? Yes, also of Gentiles, since God is indeed

One, who will justify circumcision (Jews) by faith and uncircumcision (Gentiles) through the same faith.

4:11–12: . . . This makes him (Abraham) father of all who believe
without being circumcised (Gentiles) and who thus have
righteousness reckoned to them, as well as father of the circumcised (Jews).

11:30–32: Just as you (Gentiles) were once disobedient to God, but
now have received mercy because of their (Jews') disobedience, so also they (Jews) have now been disobedient for
the benefit of the mercy shown to you (Gentiles), in order
that they (Jews) may now receive mercy. For God has imprisoned all in disobedience, in order that he may have
mercy on all!

15:8–9: For I declare that Christ became a servant of the circumcision (Jews) for the sake of God's fidelity, to confirm the
promises to the patriarchs, and that the Gentiles might glorify God for the sake of mercy.

15:27: For if the Gentiles have shared in their (Jews') spiritual
blessings, they are also indebted to minister to them in material blessings.

15:28 Once Paul has completed this most important and necessary apostolic mission and assured that the contribution to Jerusalem
has been successfully delivered and officially received, he hopes to go
on by way of his Roman readers to Spain.

15:29 And the completion of his apostolic ministry in Jerusalem
will give Paul the confident hope of knowing that when he finally arrives at Rome he will come with the fullness of the blessing of Christ.
Paul thus relays to his Roman auditors the realization that, although it
will delay his arrival in Rome, his successfully completed mission to
Jerusalem will richly benefit them, as it will enable him to bring them
the full spiritual blessing of Christ.

c. Paul requests the prayers of the Roman Christians for the successful completion of his mission to Jerusalem.

15:30 As the Christians at Rome play a strategically pivotal role
in Paul's apostolic hope for extending the gospel as far as Spain
(15:24), so they must also assist him in his apostolic hope for successfully delivering the collection to Jerusalem. Paul urgently exhorts his
Roman readers to share in his hope for the success of the Jerusalem
ministry by praying before God on his behalf. They are to join in his

hope by "striving together" with him as they actualize their hope in their prayers.[2]

15:31 The Romans are to pray that God accomplish his salvific will on Paul's behalf in Jerusalem and rescue Paul from the troublesome unbelievers in Judea, so that his service to Jerusalem be rendered acceptable to the Christian "saints" there.

15:32 Then, Paul can finally fulfill, through the will of God, his eager longing of visiting the Christians at Rome in joy and being vibrantly "refreshed" together with them, that is, of being "mutually encouraged" through their mutual Christian faith and hope (see 1:11–12; 15:24).

15:33 Paul closes his exhortation with the encouraging prayer wish that the God who gives harmonious "peace" may be with all of the Christians in Rome!

C. Rom 16:1–16: Paul Greets and Recommends Contributors and Co-Workers of His Apostolate.

Although Paul did not establish the Roman church and is not personally acquainted with the majority of Christians in Rome, there are many now present in Rome who have played auxiliary roles in Paul's past apostolic ministry. Through them Paul is enabled to draw his Roman audience closer to himself as author of the Letter and deeper into his apostolic hope for the future.

These associates of Paul now in Rome can vouch to the others of Paul's past success in bringing the gospel to its full completion in the regions from Jerusalem to Illyricum (15:17–19). They have shared in and serve as living testimony to Paul's apostolic hope of leading all nations to the "obedience of faith" (1:5; 15:18) in the gospel of hope.

Now, by introducing and recommending them to the other Christians at Rome whom he does not yet know Paul embraces his entire Roman Christian readership together in his hopeful apostolic aspiration to extend the gospel as far as Spain.

1. *Romans 16:1–16:*

1 I recommend to you our sister Phoebe, a deaconess of the church at Cenchreae, 2 that you may welcome her in the Lord in a way worthy of the saints, and assist her in whatever she needs from you, for indeed she has been a benefactress of many and of myself as well.

3 Greet Prisca and Aquila, my fellow workers in Christ Jesus, who

risked their own necks for my life, to whom not only I but all the churches of the Gentiles offer thanks; 5 greet also the church in their house. Greet Epaenetus my beloved, who is the first-fruit of Asia for Christ. 6 Greet Mary, who has labored hard for you. 7 Greet Andronicus and Junias, my kinsmen and my fellow prisoners, who are notable among the apostles, and who have been in Christ longer than I. 8 Greet Ampliatus, my beloved in the Lord. 9 Greet Urbanus, our fellow worker in Christ, and Stachys my beloved. 10 Greet Apelles, who is approved in Christ. Greet those of the household of Aristobulus. 11 Greet Herodion my kinsman. Greet those of the household of Narcissus who are in the Lord. 12 Greet Tryphaena and Tryphosa, workers in the Lord. Greet the beloved Persis, who has labored hard in the Lord. 13 Greet Rufus, eminent in the Lord, and also his mother and mine. 14 Greet Asyncritus, Phlegon, Hermes, Patrobas, Hermas, and the fellow Christians with them. 15 Greet Philologus and Julia, Nereus and his sister, and Olympas and all the saints with them. 16 Greet one another with a holy kiss. All the churches of Christ greet you!

a. The Romans should welcome and help Phoebe who had earlier assisted Paul and many others.

16:1 Paul specially commends to "you," his entire audience at Rome, a certain Phoebe, designated as "our sister," a "deaconess" or "helper" of the Christian community gathered in Cenchreae, an eastern seaport for Corinth. Since Paul is probably writing the Letter from Corinth, it may well be that Phoebe has been entrusted to deliver the Letter to the Romans and arrange for its dissemination and hearing among the various groups of Christians at Rome.

16:2 They are to receive and welcome her in the Lord as befits Christian "saints." And they should present to her whatever she needs from them for her work at hand, possibly that involved in delivering the Letter. Such assistance to her is appropriate for them since she has previously aided Paul himself and many other Christians.

b. The Romans should greet Prisca and Aquila, who risked their lives for Paul.

16:3–5 Paul bids the Christians at Rome to extend greetings to Prisca and Aquila, his fellow workers in spreading the gospel of Christ Jesus. They have previously gone so far as to risk their own lives to assist Paul in his apostolate. For this reason not only Paul himself but all the Gentile churches he has founded in the Mediterranean area owe them a debt of gratitude. Greetings should also be given to the church which now meets in their house at Rome.

According to the Acts of the Apostles Aquila was a Christian Jew who, together with his wife Prisca or Priscilla, had moved from Rome to Corinth after Claudius had commanded all the Jews to leave Rome. Paul met them while he was in Corinth, and he stayed and worked together with them at the trade of tentmaking, while he was preaching the gospel in that area (Acts 18:2).

Later, they accompanied Paul to Ephesus (Acts 18:18) and stayed there preaching the gospel (Acts 18:26), while Paul went on to Caesarea and Antioch (Acts 18:22). They evidently established and presided over a house church at Ephesus before they returned to do the same at Rome (see 1 Cor 16:19; 2 Tim 4:19).

c. The Romans should greet the various associates of Paul who are now in Rome.

16:5 Paul wishes the Roman Christians to greet Epaenetus, who, as the "first-fruit" or convert to Christ in Asia, embodies living evidence for the Romans of Paul's past missionary success.

16:6 Greetings are due Mary as one who has worked hard at the apostolate of the gospel for the Romans.

16:7 Greetings go to Andronicus and Junias as Paul's fellow Jews who were also fellow prisoners with him in the persecuting trials and tribulations of his missionary endeavor. They are notable among apostles for the gospel and even came to Christ before Paul himself.

16:8 Ampliatus is to be saluted as Paul's "beloved," an expression of an especially close relationship to Paul in his apostolate.

16:9–15 The following are to be greeted because of various associations with the missionary work of Paul: Urbanus is a fellow worker; Stachys, "my beloved"; Apelles, "proved" or "tried" in Christ; those of the household or house church of Aristobulus; Herodion, "my fellow kinsman"; those of the household or house church of Narcissus; Tryphaena and Tryphosa as missionary "workers" with Paul in the Lord; the beloved Persis who has worked hard in the Lord; Rufus as one "eminent" in the work of the Lord as well as the mother of both him and Paul; Asyncritus, Phlegon, Hermes, Patrobas, Hermas and the fellow Christians with them; Philologus, Julia, Nereus and his sister, and Olympas, and all the Christian "saints" with them.

16:16 Finally, all of Paul's Christian audience at Rome are to warmly and affectionately greet one another with "a holy kiss." And Paul, through the authority of his great apostolate, extends the greetings of all the other Christian churches to the church at Rome.

D. Rom 16:17–20: A Final Exhortation.

Although this final exhortation in the Letter may not be from Paul himself but from a later interpolator, it can be understood in relation to the message of the Letter.[3]

1. Romans 16:17–20:

17 I exhort you, fellow Christians, to look out for those who create dissensions and difficulties against the teaching which you learned, and avoid them. 18 For such persons do not serve our Lord Christ but their own bellies, and by attractive speech and flattering words deceive the hearts of the unsuspecting. 19 Your obedience has become known to all. I rejoice over you, then, but I want you to be wise as to what is good, and innocent as to what is evil. 20 The God of peace will soon crush Satan under your feet. The grace of our Lord Jesus be with you!

16:17 Paul or an interpolator vehemently warns the Roman Christians to strictly remain aloof from those enemies of the community who instigate alienating dissensions and vile difficulties in opposition to the "teaching" (see 6:17), the Christian gospel illustrated previously by Paul, that they have learned. The readers are thus aroused to a precautionary stance of keen alertness.

16:18 Such adversaries to the peace of the Christian community do not humbly "serve" (see 6:15–23; 14:7–9) our Lord Christ but selfishly serve only themselves, their own "bellies." This may allude to the same or similar problems regarding the eating of certain foods mentioned earlier in Romans 14.

Our author thus cautiously alarms his audience that by smooth and appealing talk these troublesome and dangerous opponents can deceptively lead unsuspecting Christians astray.

16:19 The author is persuasively exhorting his listeners to live in accord with their strong Christian faith and hope. The "obedience" of faith of the Roman community (see 1:5; 10:16) has become known to all (see 1:8; 15:14). While this causes the author to rejoice, he nevertheless cautions them to remain alertly "wise" as to what is of benefit, and "innocent" as to what is evil for the Christian community.

16:20 The eschatological hope that God, who is the source of harmonious "peace" for the Christian community, *will soon crush* the apocalyptic arch-enemy Satan, the source of all evil, under "your" feet is projected as the stirring motivation for the exhortation. And the prayer-wish that the grace of our Lord Jesus be with "you" adds a closing encouragement to the exhortation.

E. Rom 16:21–27: Final Greetings and Doxology.

Warm salutations from close associates of Paul bring the Letter to a close. And a final touch is provided by a rousing doxology in tune with the bright, inspiring hope enkindled by the Letter.

1. Romans 16:21–27:

21 Timothy, my fellow worker, greets you; as well as Lucius, Jason and Sosipater, my kinsmen.

22 I Tertius, who have written down the Letter, greet you in the Lord.

23 Gaius, the host of me and of the whole church, greets you. Erastus, the treasurer of the city, and our brother Quartus, greet you.

25 To him who has the power to strengthen you according to my gospel and the preaching of Jesus Christ, according to the revelation of the mystery kept secret for long ages, 26 but now manifested and made known through the prophetic writings in accord with the command of the eternal God for the obedience of faith among all the nations— 27 to the only wise God, through Jesus Christ, be glory forever. Amen!

a. Close associates of Paul greet his Roman audience.

16:21 Timothy is designated as a "fellow worker" of Paul in his apostolate of preaching the gospel. He along with Lucius, Jason and Sosipater, Jewish "kinsmen" of Paul, send their greetings to the Roman Christians.

16:22 Paul has dictated the Letter to a certain Tertius, who personally adds his own fond greeting to the readers.

16:23 Finally, Gaius, the hospitable host of Paul and of the whole Christian community gathered in the city (probably Corinth) from where Paul is sending the Letter, Erastus, the city treasurer, and Quartus, a fellow Christian "brother," greet the Christian community at Rome.

b. God is praised as the One who has the power to strengthen Christians in accord with the gospel of hope.

16:25–27 Whether or not this closing doxology belonged to the original Letter and whether or not it was composed by Paul,[4] it quite appropriately corresponds to the theme and pattern of Christian hope presented in the Letter.

It begins by addressing God as the One who possesses the "power" to "strengthen" Christians in accord with the gospel, the preaching of Jesus Christ. This aptly sums up Paul's purpose of presenting the gospel of hope in the Letter to the Romans (1:15–16) in order that they may be spiritually "strengthened" (1:11) and "encouraged" (1:12) in the hope that comes from their faith.

This spiritual "strength," an attribute of Christian hope (see 4:18–20), has its firm foundation in the gospel, which, as the definitive and decisive unfolding of the mystery kept secret for long ages but now disclosed and made evident through the prophetic writings (see 1:1–2; 3:21), according to the command of God, thus fulfills past hopes and awakens new hope.

The gospel likewise incites the broader "apostolic" hope whose future aim is the "obedience of faith among all nations" (see 1:5). This final doxology, then, lauds God for the spiritual "strength," the strong hope, that emerges from faith in the gospel, the gospel which also arouses the apostolic hope of bringing about the "obedience of faith" among all nations. In so doing, it functions as one final thrust of electrifying encouragement for the readers to have and hold this superbly vibrant hope that is theirs through their faith in the gospel of Jesus Christ.

F. Final Summary

In Rom 15:14—16:27 Paul has excitingly lured and attracted his Roman audience, who already exhibit the "obedience of faith" (1:5, 8; 15:14), to share in his apostolic hope of evangelizing where Christ has not yet been made known in order to bring about the "obedience of faith" among all nations (15:14–21). He has effectively related and encompassed his readers into his global apostolate.

Paul has informed his Roman listeners of the strategically pivotal role they are yet to enact within his global mission. He hopes to see them in person not only to be encouraged by them in their mutual hope coming from their common faith (1:11–12; 15:24, 32) but also to be supported by them in his future plan to extend the gospel as far as Spain (15:22–24), after he has successfully completed his apostolic ministry of delivering the collection of the Gentiles to Jerusalem through the much needed assistance of the Roman Christians' prayers (15:25–33). In this way Paul's Roman readers may not only share in but contribute to and effectively promote the apostolic aspiration of advancing the gospel throughout the world.

Paul calls on his auditors to warmly welcome and greet his many associates and fellow workers who are now present among the Romans. They serve as living evidence of how the gospel has spread in the past (15:17–19) and enkindle the ardent aspiration of expanding it likewise in the future—even as far as Spain (16:1–16, 21–23).

The Roman Christians have been alerted to avoid any false teaching disrupting the peace and well-being of the community (16:17–20).

With a final flamboyant surge, the concluding doxology fittingly epitomizes the Letter's overall thrust toward hope: In itself it actualizes the boldly confident hope in the God who can spiritually strengthen Christians in the hope which gushes forth from the gospel, the gospel which enkindles the burning, global hope for the "obedience of faith" among all peoples (16:25–27).

In conclusion, Paul, throughout the entire Letter, has projected a concerted effort to awaken, deepen and increase the Christian hope of his readers. From beginning to end the overall tone and tenor of the Letter has been one of encouraging and optimistic hopefulness. This rousing and ringing note of hopefulness has served as a unifying factor for the whole Letter to the Romans, which can certainly be characterized as Paul's great "letter of hope."

NOTES

1. BAGD, 709.

2. Prayer, which is oriented to the future completion of God's salvific plan, the future goal of hope, we consider to be "hope in action" or an "actualization" of the attitude of hope; see 8:26–27; 12:12.

3. According to Ollrog ("Abfassungsverhältnisse," 227, 230–234), Rom 16:17–20 may be a later interpolation added about 96 A.D. at the time that 1 Clement quoted from Romans. Gamble (*Textual History*, 52–53), however, thinks that these verses are not necessarily secondary.

4. J. K. Elliott ("The Language and Style of the Concluding Doxology to the Epistle to the Romans," *ZNW* 72 [1981] 124–130) does not think that Rom 16:25–27 was composed by Paul. And Ollrog ("Abfassungsverhältnisse," 227), following the consensus among scholars on this point, thinks it very probable that these verses are a later addition to the Letter.

Select Bibliography

Aageson, J. W. "Scripture and Structure in the Development of the Argument in Romans 9–11." *CBQ* 48 (1986) 265–289.

Achtemeier, P. J. *Romans.* Atlanta: John Knox, 1985.

Aus, R. D. "Paul's Travel Plans to Spain and the "Full Number of the Gentiles" of Rom. xi 25." *NovT* 21 (1979) 232–262.

Badenas, R. *Christ The End of the Law: Romans 10.4 in Pauline Perspective.* JSNTSup 10. Sheffield: JSOT, 1985.

Balz, H. R. *Heilsvertrauen und Welterfahrung. Strukturen der paulinischen Eschatologie nach Römer 8,18–39.* BEvT 59. Munich: Kaiser, 1971.

Banks, R. "Romans 7.25a: An Eschatological Thanksgiving?" *AusBR* 26 (1978) 34–42.

Barrett, C. K. *A Commentary on the Epistle to the Romans.* HNTC. New York: Harper & Row, 1957.

Beker, J. C. *Paul's Apocalyptic Gospel. The Coming Triumph of God.* Philadelphia: Fortress, 1982.

———. *Paul the Apostle. The Triumph of God in Life and Thought.* Philadelphia: Fortress, 1980.

Black, M. *Romans.* NCB. London: Oliphants, 1973.

Bruce, F. F. "The Romans Debate—Continued." *BJRL* 64 (1981–82) 334–359.

Byrne, B. "Living Out the Righteousness of God: The Contribution of Rom 6:1–8:13 to an Understanding of Paul's Ethical Presuppositions." *CBQ* 43 (1981) 557–581.

Campbell, W. S. "The Romans Debate." *JSNT* 10 (1981) 19–28.

———. "Revisiting Romans." *ScrB* 12 (1981) 2–10.

———. "Romans III as a Key to the Structure and Thought of the Letter." *NovT* 23 (1981) 22–40.

———. "Why Did Paul Write Romans?" *ExpTim* 85 (1973–74) 264–269.

Cavallin, H. C. C. " 'The Righteous Shall Live by Faith.' A Decisive Argument for the Traditional Interpretation." *ST* 32 (1978) 33–43.

Clements, R. E. " 'A Remnant Chosen by Grace' (Romans 11:5): The Old Testament Background and Origin of the Remnant Concept." *Pauline Studies. Essays Presented to Professor F. F. Bruce on His*

70th Birthday. Ed. D. A. Hagner and M. J. Harris. Grand Rapids: Eerdmans, 1980, 106–121.

Cranfield, C. E. B. *A Critical and Exegetical Commentary on the Epistle to the Romans.* ICC. 2 vols. Edinburgh: T. & T. Clark, 1975, 1979.

_____. *Romans: A Shorter Commentary.* Grand Rapids: Eerdmans, 1985.

Dabelstein, R. *Die Beurteilung der 'Heiden' bei Paulus.* Beiträge zur biblischen Exegese und Theologie 14. Frankfurt/Bern/Cirencester: Lang, 1981.

de Kruyf, Th. "The Perspective of Romans VII." *Miscellanea Neotestamentica.* Ed. T. Baarda, A. F. J. Klijn and W. C. Van Unnik. NovTSup 48. Leiden: Brill, 1978, 127–141.

Drane, J. W. "Why Did Paul Write Romans?" *Pauline Studies. Essays Presented to Professor F. F. Bruce on His 70th Birthday.* Ed. D. A. Hagner and M. J. Harris. Grand Rapids: Eerdmans, 1980, 208–227.

Dunn, J. D. G. "The New Perspective on Paul." *BJRL* 65 (1982–83) 95–122.

Elliott, J. K. "The Language and Style of the Concluding Doxology to the Epistle to the Romans." *ZNW* 72 (1981) 124–130.

Evans, C. A. "Romans 12.1–2: The True Worship." *Dimensions de la vie chrétienne.* Ed. L. De Lorenzi. Monographic Series of "Benedictina," Biblical-Ecumenical Section 4. Rome: St. Paul's Abbey, 1979, 7–49.

_____. "Paul and the Hermeneutics of 'True Prophecy': A Study of Romans 9–11." *Bib* 65 (1984) 560–570.

Fung, R. Y. K. "The Impotence of the Law: Toward a Fresh Understanding of Romans 7:14–25." *Scripture, Tradition, and Interpretation.* Essays Presented to E. F. Harrison. Ed. W. W. Gasque and W. S. LaSor. Grand Rapids: Eerdmans, 1978, 34–48.

Gamble, H. *The Textual History of the Letter to the Romans.* Studies and Documents 42. Grand Rapids: Eerdmans, 1977.

Hahn, F. "Zum Verständnis von Römer 11.26a: '. . . und so wird ganz Israel gerettet werden.' " *Paul and Paulinism. Essays in Honour of C. K. Barrett.* Ed. M. D. Hooker and S. G. Wilson. London: SPCK, 1982, 221–236.

Hall, D. R. "Romans 3. 1–8 Reconsidered." *NTS* 29 (1983) 183–197.

Hanson, A. T. "Vessels of Wrath or Instruments of Wrath? Romans IX. 22–3." *JTS* 32 (1981) 433–443.

Hays, R. B. "Psalm 143 and the Logic of Romans 3." *JBL* 99 (1980) 107–115.

Herold, G. *Zorn und Gerechtigkeit Gottes bei Paulus. Eine Untersuchung zu Röm. 1.16–18.* Europäische Hochschulschriften 23/14. Bern/Frankfurt: Lang, 1973.

Jewett, R. "Romans as an Ambassadorial Letter." *Int* 36 (1982) 5–20.

Johnson, D. G. "The Structure and Meaning of Romans 11." *CBQ* 46 (1984) 91–103.

Johnson, L. T. "Romans 3:21–26 and the Faith of Jesus." *CBQ* 44 (1982) 77–90.

Käsemann, E. *Commentary on Romans.* Grand Rapids: Eerdmans, 1980.

———. "The Faith of Abraham in Romans 4." *Perspectives on Paul.* London: SCM, 1971, 79–101.

Kaye, B. N. *The Thought Structure of Romans with Special Reference to Chapter 6.* Austin: Schola Press, 1979.

Kettunen, M. *Der Abfassungszweck des Römerbriefes.* Annales Academiae Scientiarum Fennicae Dissertationes Humanarum Litterarum 18. Helsinki: Suomalainen Tiedeakatemia, 1979.

Lambrecht, J. "Why Is Boasting Excluded? A Note on Rom 3,27 and 4,2." *ETL* 61 (1985) 365–369.

Lyonnet, S. "De 'Iustitia Dei' in Epistola ad Romanos." *VD* 25 (1947) 23–34, 118–121, 129–144, 193–203, 257–263.

———. *Quaestiones in Epistulam ad Romanos. Series Altera. Rom 9–11.* 3d ed. Rome: Biblical Institute, 1975.

———. "Note sur le plan de l'épître aux Romains." *RSR* 39 (1951) 301–316.

Lyons, G. *Pauline Autobiography: Toward a New Understanding.* SBLDS 73. Atlanta: Scholars, 1985.

Marrow, S. B. *Paul: His Letters and His Theology.* New York/Mahwah: Paulist, 1986.

Meeks, W. "Social Functions of Apocalyptic Language in Pauline Christianity." *Apocalypticism in the Mediterranean World and the Near East.* Ed. D. Hellholm. Tübingen: Mohr, 1983, 687–705.

Michel, O. *Der Brief an die Römer.* Meyerk 4. 14th ed. Göttingen: Vandenhoeck & Ruprecht, 1978.

Minear, P. S. *The Obedience of Faith. The Purposes of Paul in the Epistle to the Romans.* SBT 19. Naperville: Allenson, 1971.

Moo, D. J. "Israel and Paul in Romans 7.7–12." *NTS* 32 (1986) 122–135.

———. " 'Law,' 'Works of the Law,' and Legalism in Paul." *WTJ* 45 (1983) 73–100.

Moody, R. M. "The Habakkuk Quotation in Romans 1:17." *ExpTim* 92 (1981) 205–208.

Newman, B. M. "Once Again—The Question of 'I' in Romans 7.7–25." *BT* 34 (1983) 124–135.

Newman, B. M. and Nida, E. A. *A Translator's Handbook on Paul's Letter to the Romans.* New York: United Bible Societies, 1973.

Ollrog, W.-H. "Die Abfassungsverhältnisse von Röm 16." *Kirche. Festschrift für G. Bornkamm zum 75. Geburtstag.* Ed. D. Lührmann and G. Strecker. Tübingen: Mohr, 1980, 221–244.

———. *Paulus und seine Mitarbeiter. Untersuchungen zu Theorie und Praxis der paulinischen Mission.* WMANT 50. Neukirchen-Vluyn: Neukirchener Verlag, 1979.

Penna, R. "Les Juifs à Rome au temps de l'apôtre Paul." *NTS* 28 (1982) 321–347.

Popkes, W. "Zum Aufbau und Charakter von Römer 1.18–32." *NTS* 28 (1982) 490–501.

Räisänen, H. *Paul and the Law.* WUNT 29. Tübingen: Mohr, 1983.

Rhyne, C. T. *Faith Establishes the Law.* SBLDS 55. Chico: Scholars Press, 1981.

Rolland, Ph. " 'Il est notre justice, notre vie, notre salut'. L'ordonnance des thèmes majeurs de l'Epître aux Romains." *Bib* 56 (1975) 394–404.

———. *Epître aux Romains. Texte grec structuré.* Rome: Biblical Institute, 1980.

Sanders, E. P. *Paul and Palestinian Judaism.* London: SCM, 1977.

Schlier, H. *Der Römerbrief.* HTKNT 6. Freiburg/Basel/Wien: Herder, 1977.

Siegert, F. *Argumentation bei Paulus: Gezeigt an Röm 9–11.* WUNT 34. Tübingen: Mohr, 1985.

Snodgrass, K. R. "Justification by Grace—to the Doers: An Analysis of the Place of Romans 2 in the Theology of Paul." *NTS* 32 (1986) 72–93.

Stambaugh, J. E. and Balch, D. L. *The New Testament in Its Social Environment.* Library of Early Christianity 2. Philadelphia: Westminster, 1986.

Stowers, S. K. *The Diatribe and Paul's Letter to the Romans.* SBLDS 57. Chico: Scholars Press, 1981.

Webster, A. F. C. "St. Paul's Political Advice to the Haughty Gentile Christians in Rome: An Exegesis of Romans 13:1–7." *St. Vladimir's Theological Quarterly* 25 (1981) 259–282.

Wedderburn, A. J. M. "The Purpose and Occasion of Romans Again." *ExpTim* 90 (1979) 137–141.

Wiefel, W. "The Jewish Community in Ancient Rome and the Origins of Roman Christianity." *The Romans Debate.* Ed. K. P. Donfried. Minneapolis: Augsburg, 1977, 100–119.

Wilckens, U. *Der Brief an die Römer.* EKKNT 6/1–2–3. Neukirchen-Vluyn: Neukirchener Verlag, 1978, 1980, 1982.

Wiles, G. P. *Paul's Intercessory Prayers. The Significance of the Intercessory*

Prayer Passages in the Letters of St. Paul. SNTSMS 24. Cambridge: Cambridge University Press, 1974.

Williams, S. K. "The "Righteousness of God" in Romans." *JBL* 99 (1980) 241–290.

Wolter, M. *Rechtfertigung und zukünftiges Heil. Untersuchungen zu Röm 5,1–11.* BZNW 43. Berlin/New York: de Gruyter, 1978.

Wuellner, W. "Paul's Rhetoric of Argumentation in Romans: An Alternative to the Donfried—Karris Debate over Romans." *The Romans Debate.* Ed. K. P. Donfried. Minneapolis: Augsburg, 1977, 152–174.

Zerwick, M. "Drama populi Israel secundum Rom 9–11." *VD* 46 (1968) 321–338.

Index of Scripture References

Index of Subjects